things, hopeth all things; endureth all things.

8 Charity never faileth: but whether there be prophecies, they shall fail; whether there be tongues, they shall cease; whether there be knowledge, it shall vanish away.

9 For we know in part, and we prophesy in part.

10 But when that which is perfect is come, then that which is in part shall be done away.

11 When I was a child, I spake as a child, I understood as a child, I thought as a child: but when I became a man, I put away childish things.

12 For now we see through a glass, darkly; but then face to face: now I know in part; but then shall I know even as also I am known.

13 And now abideth faith, hope, charity, these three; but the greatest of these is charity.

CHARITY NEVER FAILETH

Vaughn J. Featherstone

Deseret Book Company
Salt Lake City, Utah
1980

Library of Congress Cataloging in Publication Data
Featherstone, Vaughn J
    Charity never faileth.

    Includes index.
    1.   Christian life—Mormon authors.   2.   Charity.
I.   Title.
BX8656.F4   248.4   80-10528
ISBN 0-87747-806-6

Contents

Preface   vii

Chapter One
Charity Never Faileth   1

Chapter Two
The Pure Love of Christ   8

Chapter Three
These Are Not Men to Be Conquered   17

Chapter Four
Blessed Are the Merciful   22

Chapter Five
Caring for the Aged   27

Chapter Six
The Blessing of a Mission   34

Chapter Seven
"My Sheep Hear My Voice"   41

Chapter Eight
The Impact Teacher   52

Chapter Nine
The House of the Lord   58

Chapter Ten
Time Limits   64

Chapter Eleven
Preparing Ourselves Through Prayer   69

Chapter Twelve
When Trials Come   73

Chapter Thirteen
Acres of Diamonds   82

Chapter Fourteen
Walking in His Steps   93

Chapter Fifteen
Unconditional Love   109

Index   117

Preface

The word *charity* has many meanings and is understood in a semantically different way by almost all who use it. The dictionary defines charity as "benevolent good will toward or love of humanity; kindly liberality and helpfulness especially toward the needy or suffering; aid given to those in need; an institution engaged in relief of the needy; a gift for public benevolent purposes; lenient judgment of others."

In the thirteenth chapter of First Corinthians, the apostle Paul suggests that we may do any and all of the above and still not possess true charity. The purest definition seems to be the simplest: "Charity is the pure love of Christ." (Moroni 7:47.)

The greatest, most impressive, most Christlike persons I know seem to have a special understanding of charity. It seems to me that charity is not merely an act of kindness or a contribution to aid the poor, but rather a total way of life. To be true, charity is involved in every thought and deed, and in our actual living from one moment to another. It also seems to me that in order to have charity in its fulness, a person must be a member of the Lord's true and living church. The companionship of the Holy Ghost is an essential part of having true charity.

I have known many fine people who actually had testimonies that The Church of Jesus Christ of Latter-day Saints was the true restored church of the Master, but who would not change their way of life or could not bear the criticism of their nonmember friends. Regardless of their charitable acts, such persons do not possess true charity.

Charity involves long-suffering, patience, Godly judging of our fellow beings, a forgiving heart, devotion to service, commitment to truth, inward humility, and sorrow for those who are suffering or afflicted. It is an attitude of doing what the Master would do if he were here and faced with a particular problem. It is an intense struggle to live all the commandments and not be selective. It is treating every soul with love unfeigned and dignity, to see each person as a special creation of the Almighty God of heaven. Indeed, charity is the "pure love of Chirst."

In this volume I have written chapters that, it is hoped, will lead the reader to a more intense and deeper study of charity. Those who are seeking exaltation will find that goal is unattainable without true charity. Those who do possess true charity will find that "charity never faileth." (Moroni 7:46.)

In the preparation of this book I am grateful to my secretary, Sherri McGrath, for typing and proofreading; to Eleanor Knowles, for editing the manuscript; and especially to Lowell Durham, Jr., who invited me to write the manuscript.

Chapter One

Charity Never Faileth

Recently, I decided to prepare several talks on charity. I memorized the thirteenth chapter of 1 Corinthians, understanding that when you memorize something it becomes part of you. It is always accessible for recall, and each time it is quoted to others or oneself, it has a profound impact.

Before we review this marvelous counsel and instruction from Paul, let me share a few ideas that may bring more meaning to it. For whom was it given? Although it has universal application, it appears to me that Paul may have been addressing the brethren. Possibly he even understood its great application in our day, in this the dispensation of the fullness of times. He speaks of those who have the gift of prophecy, those who understand all scriptures and have all knowledge, who have faith to move mountains, who give their all to the poor, and who sacrifice their lives.

His message, although universal, seems to be directed to those who walk in high places in the Church, men and women of great experience, great commitment—authorized agents of the Master. I think it may be a warning to all of us. We may do many great things in the kingdom following true and correct principles and then are sometimes tripped up by

1

some things that seem lesser but indeed measure a person's charity, or pure love of Christ.

Those of us who have been endowed with greater opportunities for service are expected to measure up, in great and momentous things but equally important small and seemingly insignificant qualities, to the stature of Him whose work this is.

Imagine what a blessing Moroni was to his great father. Moroni understood charity. He taught it. He lived it. Whence cometh the training that so perfectly prepared Moroni, who was filled with the pure love of Christ? It came from his great father. Listen to the instructions and tender feelings of a loving parent filled with charity:

"My beloved son, Moroni, I rejoice exceedingly that your Lord Jesus Christ hath been mindful of you, and hath called you to his ministry, and to his holy work. I am mindful of you always in my prayers, continually praying unto God the Father in the name of his Holy Child, Jesus, that he, through his infinite goodness and grace, will keep you through the endurance of faith on his name to the end." (Moroni 8:2-3.)

Then, after describing the deplorable conduct of the Nephites, Mormon said to his son: "Behold, my son, I cannot recommend them unto God lest he should smite me. But behold, my son, I recommend thee unto God, and I trust in Christ that thou wilt be saved; and I pray unto God that he will spare thy life, to witness the return of his people unto him, or their utter destruction; for I know that they must perish except they repent and return unto him." (Moroni 9:21-22.)

"And I am filled with charity, which is everlasting love; wherefore, all children are alike unto me; wherefore, I love little children with a perfect love; and they are all alike and partakers of salvation." (Moroni 8:17.)

We remember that Mormon led the Nephites as general over all the armies when he was sixteen, but he was still the general over all the armies when he was seventy-four. Again, he said to Moroni: "And now, my beloved son, notwithstanding their hardness, let us labor diligently; for if we should cease to labor, we should be brought under condemnation; for we have a labor to perform whilst in this tabernacle of clay, that we may conquer the enemy of all righteousness, and rest our souls in the kingdom of God.

"And now I write somewhat concerning the sufferings of this people. For according to the knowledge which I have received from Amoron, behold, the Lamanites have many prisoners, which they took from the tower of Sherrizah; and there were men, women, and children." (Moroni 9:6-7.)

At the conclusion of his labors with the Gentiles Moroni wrote: "And now I, Moroni, bid farewell unto the Gentiles, yea, and also unto my brethren whom I love, until we shall meet before the judgment-seat of Christ, where all men shall know that my garments are not spotted with your blood. And then shall ye know that I have seen Jesus, and that he hath talked with me face to face, and that he told me in plain humility, even as a man telleth another in mine own language, concerning these things." (Ether 12:38-39.)

These scriptures thrill us almost unto the consuming of the soul, as we feel the love of Christ through them. And now, once again, let us return to Paul's discourse on charity:

"Though I speak with the tongues of men and of angels and have not charity, I am become as sounding brass, or a tinkling cymbal.

"And though I have the gift of prophecy, and understand all mysteries, and all knowledge; and though I have all faith, so that I could remove mountains, and have not charity, I am nothing.

"And though I bestow all my goods to feed the poor, and though I give my body to be burned, and have not charity, it profiteth me nothing.

"Charity suffereth long, and is kind; charity envieth not;

3

charity vaunteth not itself, is not puffed up.

"Doth not behave itself unseemly, seeketh not her own, is not easily provoked, thinketh no evil;

"Rejoiceth not in iniquity, but rejoiceth in the truth;

"Beareth all things, believeth all things, hopeth all things, endureth all things.

"Charity never faileth: but whether there be prophecies, they shall fail; whether there be tongues, they shall cease; whether there be knowledge, it shall vanish away.

"For we know in part, and we prophesy in part.

"But when that which is perfect is come, then that which is in part shall be done away.

"When I was a child, I spake as a child, I understood as a child, I thought as a child: But when I became a man, I put away childish things.

"For now we see through a glass, darkly; but then face to face: now I know in part; but then shall I know even as also I am known.

"And now abideth faith, hope, charity, these three; but the greatest of these is charity." (1 Corinthians 13.)

Nephi gives additional light on this subject. He writes: "Do ye not remember that I said unto you that after ye had received the Holy Ghost ye could speak with the tongue of angels? And now, how could ye speak with the tongue of angels save it were by the Holy Ghost? Angels speak by the power of the Holy Ghost; wherefore, they speak the words of Christ. Wherefore, I said unto you, feast upon the words of Christ; for behold, the words of Christ will tell you all things what ye should do." (2 Nephi 32:2-3.)

And what about those who speak by this power and with charity?

"I have charity for my people, and great faith in Christ that I shall meet many souls spotless at his judgment-seat.

"I have charity for the Jew—I say Jew, because I mean them from whence I came.

4

"I also have charity for the Gentiles. But behold, for none of these can I hope except they shall be reconciled unto Christ, and enter into the narrow gate, and walk in the straight path which leads to life, and continue in the path until the end of the day of probation.

"And now, my beloved brethren, and also Jew, and all ye ends of the earth, hearken unto these words and believe in Christ; and if ye believe not in these words believe in Christ. And if ye shall believe in Christ ye will believe in these words, for they are the words of Christ, and he hath given them unto me; and they teach all men that they should do good.

"And if they are not the words of Christ, judge ye—for Christ will show unto you, with power and great glory, that they are his words, at the last day; and you and I shall stand face to face before his bar; and ye shall know that I have been commanded of him to write these things, notwithstanding my weakness.

"And I pray the Father in the name of Christ that many of us, if not all, may be saved in his kingdom at that great and last day.

"And now, my beloved brethren, all those who are of the house of Israel, and all ye ends of the earth, I speak unto you as the voice of one crying from the dust; Farewell until that great day shall come.

"And you that will not partake of the goodness of God, and respect the words of the Jews, and also my words, and the words which shall proceed forth out of the mouth of the Lamb of God, behold, I bid you an everlasting farewell, for these words shall condemn you at the last day.

"For what I seal on earth, shall be brought against you at the judgment bar; for thus hath the Lord commanded me, and I must obey. Amen." (2 Nephi 33:7-15.)

Charity is a total submission to the Savior's will. It is the total commitment of the soul. When the Holy Ghost pervades every particle of our being, we are filled with an awe and

5

respect for all God's creations, even to the lowliest form of animal life. Much of that which we supposed was "sport" no longer has excitement or pleasure.

And if we have such marvelous respect for God's creation, shall we not stand in absolute wonder at a man, a woman, or a child? Charity may cause us to detest what they do, but we can never cease to strive with them. We can look to their faults and be patient and forgiving because charity suffereth long and is kind. We forgive offenses, realizing that to forgive is a divine communication.

Charity appears to overcome the communication barrier so that we "know even as we are known." We can see into each heart as though it were transparent crystal. It must be the power to discern by the Spirit.

To those with heavy hearts, charity suggests that we bear all things. We may be lacking in charity if we have patience only for a short season. Remember, charity suffereth long and is kind.

Charity seeketh not her own. It would appear from this statement that we must have all the false pride stripped from our souls. We aren't concerned about saving face so much as saving souls. This means we should have an attitude of "washing of feet" in our daily walks of life. Charity causes us to become a man or a woman and to put away childish things. Our own appetites and interests are sublimated for a greater work. For a priesthood leader or a missionary it suggests that we draw nigh unto death should even one soul be lost at the last day.

Charity means to put on our beautiful garments to become saviors on Mount Zion, and to walk in paths of service normally obscured from our sight by shades of less worthy things. It means that we make ourselves totally available for service, that we realize we were born to serve our fellowmen, that we remember that we are God's agents to do his work.

Now there are many sides of charity, and it is doubtful that we can achieve this great quality in a lifetime, but we must do it in an eternity or else it will not be well with us. We have walked with men who come near the mark. President Spencer W. Kimball is such a man. Put the test to his life. Go through chapter 13 of 1 Corinthians and measure him under each variation of charity, and he is nigh unto perfect in this generation. We also can accomplish this. We can purge every unworthy thought from our hearts and souls so that our hearts may be as transparent as crystal for others to view into.

There are great principles in the Church, such as the principles of faith and hope, but there is no greater principle than charity. In The Church of Jesus Christ of Latter-day Saints we have a responsibility that cannot be found outside the Church, and that is, to possess the totality of charity. The Holy Ghost as a permanent companion is denied to all those outside the Church, as are the gifts of prophecy and of speaking in tongues. This pure and total charity must be found in the kingdom of God only, and as we possess it we put on our beautiful garments. Remember, charity abideth forever and is the pure love of Christ, which never faileth.

Chapter Two

The Pure Love of Christ

Surely the Lord places in the heart of man an upward reach. Spirituality enlarges a man's soul. The truth of that concept was impressed upon my mind some years ago when I was on the Priesthood Missionary Committee of the Church and had the privilege of being assigned to a stake conference in Pocatello, Idaho, with President Marion G. Romney, who at that time was a member of the Council of the Twelve. Between sessions of conference we went outside to get some fresh air. We walked several times around the parking lot; then President Romney stopped and said to me, "Brother Featherstone, do you think the brethren of the priesthood will ever come to understand that they were born to serve their fellowmen?" That question has had a profound impact on my life.

A Christlike love is essential if we are to serve well. Someone has said, "The only slavery is service without love." There is no substitute for pure love in our families, in our church callings, and in our dealings with our fellowmen.

A friend of mine who has been on several high councils and in a stake presidency moved to a small town in California when he was twelve or thirteen years of age. There was no ward or branch in that community. There was not a father in the home, so the mother said, "George, we are going to go to church every week. Since there isn't a Mormon church, we are going to go to the Lutheran church." So every Sunday they went to the Lutheran church.

Approximately three years after the move George came home from school one day to find his mother excited, tears of joy in her eyes. She announced that a branch of the Church had been organized, and that the branch president had come to their home. She ushered George into the living room and introduced him to a fine young man who had been called as the branch president. He shook hands with George and told him how delighted he was to have him in the branch. "You are the only boy of Aaronic Priesthood age in the branch," he said. "We really need you." George replied, "Mother, I believe the Mormon church is true, but all of my friends go down to the Lutheran church. I am going to keep going there." The mother did everything she could to get him to change his mind, but to no avail. George had decided. Each Sunday morning George and his mother would get up early and go their separate ways, she to the little rented room where the Latter-day Saints were meeting, and he in the opposite direction to the large, beautiful chapel of the Lutherans.

During the next several weeks, George recalled, he would often be on his way home from school and "just happen" to run into the branch president, leaning against a tree. "Which way are you going, George?" "To the drugstore and then home." "That is the way I am going. Do you mind if I come along?" He said that the branch president would buy him a soda at the drugstore and talk to him about how much he was needed in the branch. Each time George would say, "Well, maybe later, but not now." George told me, "I can't tell you how many times over the next several weeks that I 'just happened' to meet the branch president—at least two or three times every week. Each time he was going my direction and we would talk."

9

After many weeks had passed, one Sunday morning George got ready as usual and went to the Lutheran church. After the Sunday services were over, he and his friends stood halfway down a long stairway that led from the chapel. The minister came out of the chapel, dressed in his ministerial robes, and started shaking hands with those on the stairs. He worked his way down to where the boys were standing and shook each one by the hand. When he came to George, he said, "What is your name?" "George." "You must be new around here, I don't believe I have seen you before. Is this your first time here?" George replied, "No, it isn't my first time. I have been coming here every Sunday for three years, but this is my last time." With that, he walked down the stairs and headed in the direction of the building where the Latter-day Saints were meeting. When he arrived, he went into the foyer and looked in. There was a seat in the back row, so he quietly walked in. As he sat down, he looked up on the stand and his eyes met the eyes of the branch president. The president's eyes filled with tears. Why? Because he felt the love of the Master for every single sheep in his flock.

Schubert is said to have told a friend that his creative process consisted of remembering a melody neither he nor anyone else had ever heard before. Maybe in a similar way, to love every soul we meet is remembering a covenant we have made that neither he nor we recall in this life.

To truly love in a Christlike way demands that we strip from ourselves every particle of false pride. I like the following illustration: A young father scolded and paddled his little four-year-old son who had gotten into some mischief. The father sent the son to his bedroom. After a period of time had passed the father went upstairs to his son's bedroom. His son was sitting in the window seat with his favorite stuffed animal and some of his other toys. When he saw his father, he took all of his toys in his arms, pulled them up to his chest, and said, "These are the things that I love most." This was somewhat of a putdown to the father. He crossed the room, took his son up in his arms, and held him close in a hug. Then the son said, "But Daddy, I love you most of all." Truly the spirit of section 121 of the Doctrine and Covenants!

There are times when the absence of love just about breaks one's heart. A convert to the Church was sharing his life story with me. When he was five and his little sister was three, the parents decided they no longer wanted the children. They were turned over to a children's home for orphans. All they had were the clothes they wore and a rag doll that the little girl clutched desperately. The caretaker of the home tried to separate Andy and his little sister, but she started to cry and clung fiercely to her brother. Finally the caretaker said, "If you don't stop crying and come with me, I'll take your doll away." The little girl stopped crying, clung to her doll, and followed the woman to the girls' dormitory. Andy was taken to a boys' dormitory and assigned to a bed. That night at about eleven o'clock, as only a three-year-old child could, the little girl slipped out of bed and somehow made her way through the halls to the boys' dormitory. She managed to find Andy, and climbed in bed beside him. He snuggled around her and she quickly fell sound asleep. Only a few minutes later during a bed check the matron found the girl's bed empty and immediately surmised her whereabouts. She went to Andy's bed and found them sleeping soundly, contentedly together. She took the despairing little soul away from her brother, and Andy said, "That was the last time I ever saw her."

I am more grateful for God's pure love than I can tell you. It must break his heart when he sees some of his precious little ones who never feel loving arms and tender kisses and sweet words for good little deeds.

Some time ago I read about Sir Walter Scott. He was the gentleman's gentleman of his day. He was never unkind or inconsiderate. Little children quickly gathered at his feet when he entered the room. Adults were always anxious to be in his presence. He was extremely well mannered to all children and adults, courteous at all times, and truly one of the

11

great noble men of his generation. A friend asked Sir Walter Scott where he had been taught courtesy, manners, respect, and love. "Were you instructed at a special academy or by a private tutor, or did your mother teach you?" Sir Walter Scott replied, "When I was a boy about thirteen I saw a dog about fifty feet away. I picked up a large stone and threw it at the dog, trying to hit it but never supposing that I would. I hit the dog and broke its leg. After it had been hit the dog crawled up to me and licked my boots. I have tried since that day to have that same deep abiding love for every soul."

We had an elder in our mission who had some financial difficulties. During an interview I asked him how he was getting along financially. Tears came to his eyes and he said, "My father picked up a second job doing custodial work to earn a few extra dollars. Because that wasn't quite enough my mother went to work in the school-lunch program so she could be home when the children were, then go to work and be back home before they were out of school. Between them they are sending me ____ dollars each month. I'm doing my best, but I can't quite make it. I think they sense this at home. My little sister had a birthday and got a dollar in an envelope. She sent her birthday dollar to me because she felt I might need it." He said, "President, I'm doing the best I can to hold costs down. I haven't eaten for three days." I reached in my wallet and gave him one hundred dollars that a choice friend of mine had asked me to share with someone I felt needed it. The little sister probably could not define *love* but she knows how to live it.

Another person who knows how to serve as the Savior would have us serve is Claudia Mitton, whom we knew when we lived some years ago in Boise, Idaho. One of my assignments in the Church was as chairman of the stake finance committee. One night as I went from home to home working on finances, I called at a home where the wife was a member of the Church but her husband was not. When I went in, the man showed me around the house, which was clean and spotless. I asked if his wife was home. He said, "No, she is in the hospital and has been there for six weeks." I began to compliment him on the way his house looked, telling him how pleased his wife would be that he had kept things so well cared for. "Do you know Claudia Mitton?" he asked me. I said, "Yes, she is our ward Relief Society president." He then told me, "She is the greatest Christian woman I know. She comes over here two or three times every week and goes through my house to clean it. I have seen her down on her hands and knees scrubbing my kitchen floor. With my wife in the hospital and the heavy concerns I have for her, what a blessing it is to know that there are women like Claudia Mitton."

Let me share a few other illustrations that may enlarge our understanding of charity. At one time I was the corporate training director for a large grocery chain. I attended a business conference in Anaheim, California, where one of the speakers was a man named Mike Vance, who was the training director for the Disney Corporation.

As part of his remarks, he mentioned a group of Vietnamese war heroes who were in the United States convalescing from dismemberment and other serious injuries. The Disney Corporation had the men brought to Disneyland aboard *Mickey Mouse One*. They spent a full day there and were excited and thrilled by the experience. It finally came time for them to return by bus to the airport to board the plane for their return flight to northern California. That's when things became a little sticky. It was time to say goodbye, but there stood a group of men with hooks instead of hands, and no one knew how to say goodbye. Suddenly one of the guides, a beautiful girl named Sasha, walked up to each of the men, took his metal hook in her hand, and said, "Let me shake your hooks, fellows." She went around and shook each of their hooks one by one, and the other guides fell in line and did the same. The war heroes left with a special feeling.

Several weeks later the Disney Corporation received a thank-you letter from the commander of the injured men. He told what a great experience it had been for the men to fly on the jet, and what marvelous thrills they had had at Disneyland. "But," said he, "the thing that impressed my men most was the little girl named Sasha who wanted to shake hands with their hooks."

That is charity. Those who can develop that kind of charity are always at ease in any kind of circumstance, for we think of what the Savior would do.

Many years ago I taught a Sunday School class of teenagers. One lesson particularly impressed me. I've forgotten the title, but I've never forgotten one of the stories in the lesson.

The story is told of Abram and Zimri, two brothers who worked side by side in the field. Abram had a wife and seven sons, and Zimri had no wife or sons. When harvest time came they divided the sheaves of the harvest equally. That night after the harvest was complete, Abram sat by his warm fire with his wife and sons and thought, "It isn't right that we share equally. I have a wife and seven sons and my brother Zimri has none. I will go out and remove a generous third of the sheaves from my harvest and place them on Zimri's." So out into the night Abram went. He removed a generous third of the sheaves from his harvest and placed them on Zimri's. Then he returned to his home, content with his deed.

That night Zimri sat in his home, and as he warmed himself by the fire he thought, "It isn't fair that we share alike, for my brother Abram has a wife and seven sons and I have none. I will go out and remove a generous third of the sheaves from my harvest and place them on Abram's harvest." So out into the night Zimri went; he placed a generous third of the sheaves from his harvest onto Abram's, and then he returned to his home.

The next morning when the brothers went to work, both were astonished to see that the harvests had indeed not changed—they were equal. That night after work, when darkness had settled upon the farm, Abram again sneaked out into the night and removed a generous third of the sheaves from his

14

harvest and placed them on Zimri's. He then went to a nearby ditch to hide and see what would happen. Soon he saw the door of Zimri's house open. He saw Zimri come out into the night and begin to remove a generous third of the sheaves from his harvest and carry them over to Abram's. Abram jumped forth, ran to his brother, fell on his neck, kissed him, and wept, but he could not speak. Neither could Zimri, for both their hearts were full.

A few years ago while on a stake conference assignment I visited and spoke to Latter-day Saints in the military service at Fort Sill, Oklahoma. There I met Chaplain John Cooper, who told me that his father had been a stake president in Logan, Utah, for something like fourteen years. During those years the father had kept a guest book, and after he passed away, that book was given to his son. Chaplain Cooper asked me to sign it. I did so, and then I thumbed through the pages. There were the signatures of the Brethren from the days when two of them would travel to each stake quarterly conference, then when one visited each conference, and then when one visited every other conference. Most of the General Authorities had signed the book. As I went through it, I saw President Spencer W. Kimball's name. Date: 1954. Name: Spencer W. Kimball. Position or title: apostle. Hobby: "I love people." I thumbed through many more pages and then I saw President Kimball's name again. Date: 1964. Name: Spencer W. Kimball. Title: apostle. Hobby: "I love people."

We have leading the Church today a prophet who truly measures in word and deed to the standard of the "Man of Christ." This seems so appropriate to me as we prepare a generation to live with the Savior on this earth.

Let us as brothers and sisters in this magnificent Church love each other with the pure love of the Master. Let us begin at home with our wives and husbands, our children, and then let us extend it to our friends and neighbors. Let us love our nonmember friends with that special holy love which crashes through barricades of prejudice and misunderstanding. I know

15

that the pure love of Christ is charity, and that charity covereth a multitude of sins. I also bear witness that this is his church and we of all the souls on the earth should be recognized for our love for him and his children.

Chapter Three

These Are Not Men to Be Conquered

The act of charity is oftentimes confused with meekness, lowliness, and submissiveness. Not so. Sometimes the greatest acts of charity are those that seem cruel or harsh at the time.

Throughout the history of the world we find acts of strong men that truly have been charitable. In the face of opposition and loneliness and oftentimes great criticism, men who have had the courage to move forward and act have become men of great character and nobility. Theirs are acts of true charity also, and they ought to be numbered among the charitable.

It is told of Spinola and Richardet, ambassadors sent by the king of Spain to negotiate a treaty at the Hague in 1608, that one day they saw eight or ten persons land from a little boat and, sitting down upon the grass, proceed to make a meal of bread, cheese, and drink. "Who are those travelers?" asked the ambassadors of a peasant. "These are our worshipful masters, the deputies from the state," was the reply. Spinola whispered, "We must make peace: These are not men to be conquered." (From Samuel Smiles, *Happy Homes and the Hearts That Make Them.*)

Some time ago I had the privilege of attending a stake conference in the company of President Spencer W. Kimball, be-

17

fore he became president of the Church. Elder Kimball worked tirelessly holding one meeting after another until late Saturday night. On Sunday we held a meeting with bishoprics and high councilors at eight A.M. This was followed by the general session, a meeting with the seventies quorum, an interview with the patriarch, and the dedication of a chapel, with a talk to seminary students in the evening. We went to the stake president's home about nine o'clock to wait for our plane, which did not leave until nearly eleven. The stake president's wife wanted to fix us dinner, but Elder Kimball said, "Please, all I need is a bowl of milk and some of your homemade bread to break up in it." These are not men to be conquered.

Most men of President Kimball's stature and leadership capacity would feast on pheasant, caviar, and other sumptuous foods fit for a king. They would fill their stomachs on champagne, liquor, and wine and indulge to a point of inebriation and simplemindedness. Those who run the swiftest race, who climb the highest mountains, who swim the most dangerous streams in life are the lean and hard, the conditioned, the men of discipline and will power. These are not men to be conquered.

We have read of political leaders and business executives who glut themselves every night and sleep until ten o'clock every morning—and who soon lose their power. The law of the harvest is absolute. Someone has said that "those who dive to the depths of pleasure come up with more sand than pearls."

The story was told of Antigonus, general of Alexander the Great, who was preparing to have his army attack the enemy. The plan was devised, the strategy decided, and the hour determined. The army of General Antigonus was greatly outnumbered. When the hour arrived for the attack, word was sent to the front lines, but no one attacked. In fact, the men were about ready to retreat ingloriously. General Antigonus asked what the problem was. The captains replied that they were outnumbered so severely that the men dared not attack. General Antigonus thought for a moment and then said, "How many do you count me for?" This spirit spread through the ranks; his army attacked and won a great battle.

How many do you think the Lord counts each of his righteous servants for? How many do you count a Spencer W. Kimball for? How about a Nathan Eldon Tanner, a Marion G. Romney, or an Ezra Taft Benson?

These are not men to be conquered. When you make your contribution in life, will men list your assets and fortune or will they talk about your character and integrity?

The decline and fall of Rome were attributable to the general corruption of its people and to their engrossing love of pleasure and idleness, work in the latter days of Rome being regarded only as fit for slaves. The citizens ceased to pride themselves on the virtues of their great forefathers, and the empire fell because it did not deserve to live. And so the nations that are idle and luxurious must inevitably die out, and laborious, energetic nations take their place.

In the above statement we could replace the word *nation* with *men* and the principle would still remain the same. Men and women of principle are not easily conquered.

President Tanner had not yet reached his peak as one of Canada's great leaders. The whole world of opportunity and financial wealth perhaps beyond his wildest dreams lay ahead. Then a call came from the prophet, and it was all laid aside. President Romney sat through the funeral service of his wife on Monday, March 12, 1979. On Tuesday this great soul attended and spoke at the Logan Temple dedication. These are not men to be conquered.

Listen to the voice of one from the past who qualified as one not to be conquered. Speaking at general conference in October 1942, President J. Reuben Clark, a member of the First Presidency, said: "Now I would like to say something else, brethren, again by way of counsel. I shall be accused, when I do, of talking politics, and perhaps on this point I may

19

say I do not read anonymous letters. When they come in I just throw them into the wastebasket. I only read enough of the signed scurrilous letters that are sent to know that they are scurrilous, and then they follow along. So it is useless for anyone to try to take out any personal feeling in that way.

"You and I have heard all our lives that the time may come when the Constitution may hang by a thread. I do not know whether it is a thread or a small rope by which it now hangs, but I do know that whether it shall live or die is now in the balance.

"I have said to you before, brethren, that to me the Constitution is a part of my religion. In its place it is just as much a part of my religion as any other part. It is a part of my religion because it is one of those institutions which God has set up for His own purposes, and, as one of the brethren said today, set up so that this Church might be established, because under no other government in the world could the Church have been established as it has been established under this government.

"I think I would be safe in saying that my fellowship with you in the Church depends upon whether or not I accept the revelations and the principles which God has revealed. If I am not willing to do that, then I am not entitled to fellowship. Anyone else who fails to accept the revelations and the principles which God has revealed stands in precisely the same situation." (*Conference Report,* October 1942, p. 58.)

Isn't that a powerful declaration? I have a very strong feeling that the Lord has sent a wonderful generation of youth who will not be men and women to be conquered. What a destiny is theirs! What a marvelous period of the world in which to live! I pray that I might be able to live long enough to see many of this generation of Latter-day Saint youth stand tall, that all might come to know that these are not men and women to contend with or to be conquered. They will do and see done deeds the likes of which have never been accomplished in all of humanity. But they must be lean and hard. They must be fit for the race. They must place character, integrity, and principles of truth as the guiding lights for the dark days ahead. It thrills me to see in my mind, as it were in vision, the future greatness that awaits those who are pure and true to the teachings and example of the Master.

I pray the Lord to bless every single youth and young adult in his great church.

Chapter Four

Blessed Are the Merciful

In the Sermon on the Mount, the Savior said, "Blessed are the merciful: for they shall obtain mercy." (Matthew 5:7.) This direct reference to mercy, which is an extension of love oftentimes satisfying justice and bringing sweet forgiveness and refreshment to a tired and weary soul, is again a measure of charity.

In life every day we witness acts that reflect the Master's teachings. In this chapter I would like to speak about one segment of our society, a "special people" who seem to be endowed with compassion and love from on high. It has been my privilege to quietly observe them over the years. They come in all sizes, shapes, and assorted intelligences, but they always come. They seem to know that the Lord's work best gets done by those who do it for him. We were born to serve our fellowmen.

I speak of doctors, nurses, attendants, parents, children—those who truly are nursing fathers and mothers to all. Each one of us knows someone who has had a mongoloid child, someone with cerebral palsy, a lingering illness, a sick mind, a mutilated body, or paralyzed limbs, or who has a sick parent or child. It is impossible for those of us who have not been totally dependent on someone else to understand the love that can be given by those who become God's attendants to his special children.

I have watched mature parents love and care for snowy-crowned ones lying in hospital beds or at home. Some, unable to feed themselves, must be spoonfed every mouthful. Some must be changed as readily and often as infants have their diapers changed. Some cannot speak, but communicate with whatever signs they can make with the wrinkle of the brow or the blink of an eye. Some of these wonderful Samaritans labor long to work out the most elemental systems of communication.

Many who have lingering illness have twenty-four-hour-a-day "angel watchers," the numerous souls who perform a silent vigil through the long hours of the night, when a moment seems as an hour and a night seems forever. Every cough, change of breathing, or slightest movement by the sick one brings the vigilant one to duty.

It is not a pretty sight to see a person who has been so immaculate and impeccable in manner, dress, and eating habits deteriorate to such an extent that paralysis of the facial muscles has left him without ability to notice food or saliva drooling from the corners of his mouth. Many modest, proud, and independent persons are brought low through disease and illness. Oftentimes their extreme modesty causes even greater mental pain and anguish. Baths, shots, and care leave them stripped of their last stronghold of dignity and modesty.

Can anyone imagine the Savior's love for those who suffer thus? To those who watch carefully and silently, attending to every need of a loved one, we say, "God bless you. We love you. The Savior loves you. Your work is his work. Never despair."

I recently heard about a letter written to a national newspaper columnist. The writer said she was a nurse but was resigning. Her work had led her into child-abuse centers. Each time an abused child was brought in, her heart would nearly break. Poor, tiny, bruised, battered, mutilated children would

23

be brought in for medical attention. This is perhaps the most disgusting of all man's inhumanity to man. The case that seemed to leave the nurse no alternative but to resign was that of a little girl of only five who was brought to the center beaten almost to death by a mother who said, "I didn't know I was hitting her so hard." The child died in the nurse's arms. Just before dying the little one looked up into the nurse's eyes and said, "My mommy says I am a bad girl."

Oh, my little one, you aren't bad! I believe God sent the most special of all his angels to bring this one back. I wonder if he didn't hold her a little longer than normal. I suppose there are deeds committed by parents against their little children that cause even God to shudder.

To all the world we proclaim that there is unacceptable conduct. Justice will eventually and finally be satisfied. There will be an accounting day. We beg and plead with you—please don't mistreat your little ones. Repent of this vile evil. It would be better that you be drowned in the depths of the sea than to offend one of these little ones.

Children have such special needs. In the great plan of life every child has a mother and a father, but far too many parents abandon their God-given role. They sin, become immoral and unfaithful, seek personal pleasure—and offend God's little ones. They abdicate their sacred trust by becoming lazy and failing to provide even the barest necessities. Too often they drift through the filthy waters of self-indulgence and sins that pollute the very soul. I promise, in the sacred name of Jesus Christ, that all parents—every wife and mother, every husband and father—will stand before the bar of justice and account for their sacred family stewardship. Each will receive his or her just reward. Woe unto them by whom offenses come.

What manner of man could ever strike a woman? There is such a thing as unacceptable conduct. It is inconceivable to me that any male who professes to be a man could stoop to such vile practices. A person who would do such a thing should not be called a man. He may be a coward, a mean instrument,

24

immature, and a disgrace to the human race, but he is not a man. Any male member of the Church who would do such detestable things should be interviewed by the bishop to determine if a Church court should be held. And who attends to an abused or beaten wife? Those "angel watchers" mentioned earlier. They are there to repair broken bodies and comfort broken hearts. They oftentimes become the lifeline for those with whom they serve.

No woman in the Church should conduct herself in such a way as to be uncouth, profane, immodest, or of a base nature. On the other hand, who can describe in words the majesty and marvel of God's most beautiful creation, a true woman? A virtuous, upright woman may not receive any great notoriety, but her good deeds cause a nation to tremble. Every good woman has a Christlike love that comes near the full measure.

In our ward a few years ago, a mother answered her phone one day, and in the brief moment that she was distracted, her three-year-old daughter disappeared. The mother quickly looked around the house, then outside, and then in terror dashed to the neighbor's swimming pool. The child had toddled next door and somehow tumbled into the pool. Her mother saw her on the bottom of the pool at the deep end. Though the mother did not know how to swim, she jumped into the water and struggled desperately for the bottom of the pool, but simply did not know how to get down there. A neighbor heard the splashing and quickly ran to the pool. Finding the woman head down struggling with all her might to reach the bottom, he quickly dove in and pulled her to the surface. After pulling her to the pool's edge, he went back down after the child. In only a moment he brought her to the surface. They worked over the little soul frantically, but it was too late. The mother's life had been saved. However, knowing her, if the neighbor had not been there to pull her from the pool, I do not think she would be alive today. I believe she would not have come up from the bottom without her child.

What a stark contrast between two of God's noblest

25

creations—a woman gladly willing to give her life for her child and another beating the child cruelly and finally to death. There were angels on the other side of the veil to greet both of these little souls and take them back to a kind, loving Father, who must have cradled each of them at his bosom for a few precious moments.

Jesus said, "And whoso shall receive one such little child in my name receiveth me. But whoso shall offend one of these little ones which believe in me, it were better for him that a millstone were hanged about his neck, and that he were drowned in the depth of the sea." (Matthew 18:5-6.)

How very like little children are the mentally retarded, the paralyzed, those who have become senile, those who are afflicted with divers diseases, crippling accidents, intense suffering, and pain. I love Jesus Christ for many reasons, but my love is unbounded for his mercy. I love him for his tender, sensitive awareness of the woman with an issue of blood for twelve years who "but desired to touch the hem of his garment"; for his inexpressible pity and compassion on the widow of Nain; for his acute awareness of the leprous, the blind, the halt, and the maimed. The healing balm of his precious love and service to the sick, the weary, the tired, the afflicted, and the abused gives us the supreme example of care for the unfortunate.

To those who care without restraint, who give service in distasteful kinds of situations, who watch through the long, dark hours of the night, who lift and carry, who bathe and clean, who never seem to tire, we love you. Yours is a special act of the Savior's love. His was a healing mission; yours is a healing work. His was a mission of compassion and service; so also is yours. He loved those who have great trials and heavy hearts. And he loves you because you are an extension of his love to the unfortunate. God bless the doctors, nurses, attendants, the angels of mercy who bring such tender care to his children. May you be endowed with a compensating blessing for every act of kindness to one of the Lord's "special souls."

26

Chapter Five

Caring for the Aged

To be old and poor is to be alone, afraid, and ill-fed, and unknown. In a series of articles in November 1972, the *Wall Street Journal* discussed the problems related to the care of the aged. Following are some quotations from these articles:

"Many of the aged are gnawed by the fear not that they will die, but that they will die unnoticed by anyone."

"The poor never saved for rainy days because it rained every day of their lives."

Shabby apartments attract the elderly due to their meager incomes. Most of these people live alone "as do five million of the total U.S. population over 65. Coupled with their sense of uselessness, their solitude breeds despair."

"So, many of the elderly eat what they can get, or afford, not what is good for them. . . . Some live mainly on what they can buy from the vending machines in their hotel or apartment lobbies. . . . Others eat dog food. 'They can get two meals out of a can,' says Robert Forst."

It may be interesting to note that in the United States there are over three hundred organizations representing the interests of the aged.

I believe the Savior had great insight into problems such as this, for as he describes in his parable of the rich man and Lazarus, Lazarus was laid daily at the gate, "desiring to be fed with the crumbs which fell from the rich man's table: moreover the dogs . . . licked his sores." (Luke 16:19-21.) Both examples are pitiful plights of humanity.

Beset by problems, the elderly poor still cling fiercely to their pride; many will not ask relatives for extra help. They don't want to be a burden.

The Church is not without its fault in the care of the aged. This is not due to the principles or the teachings of the Church, but rather to the shortcomings of its members. I sat in a conference some years ago when Elder Matthew Cowley said, "A mother can take care of seven children, but seven children will not later take care of that same mother." The Church has the solution to all of life's problems. The Savior did not leave us without direction in caring for our wonderful senior Saints. He was our model. You recall his beautiful, compassionate experience with the widow in the city of Nain. (See Luke 7:11-15.)

Several years ago we lived in Garden Grove, California. I was a produce supervisor for a large grocery chain. One day I dropped by home and picked up my young son Lawrence, who was three at the time. We went out to visit a farm to see if we could procure produce for that company. I went into the sheds and examined the produce; then I was told that Jack, the farmer, was in the house. I went to the front door and rang the bell. A little lady, probably eighty-five years old, white-haired, frail, stood in the doorway.

"Is Jack here?" I asked.

"No, he isn't. His father just passed away, and he went to the hospital," she said, and then she began to weep.

I said, "Are you Jack's mother?"

She replied, "Yes."

"I'm terribly sorry about your husband." And then I was no longer a produce buyer; I was a high priest in the Church, and I said to her, "Do you believe in the resurrection?"

28

"I guess so."

And I said, "The Savior said, 'I am the resurrection, and the life: he that believeth in me, though he were dead, yet shall he live.' [John 11:25.] And 'In my Father's house are many mansions; if it were not so, I would have told you.' " (John 14:2.) And I went on with several scriptures about the resurrection.

Then finally, as I concluded I said, "Your husband will live again. He will be resurrected. Do you believe that?" I couldn't tell whether she did or not; I just knew she wasn't comforted. So I asked her, "Do you believe in prayer?"

She said, "I used to pray, but lately if I get down on my knees I can't get back up again. When I do pray, I forget what I'm supposed to pray about. And then when I'm down on my knees and no one comes, I just have to wait until someone does come."

"Would you like Lawrence and me to pray for you?"

"Yes."

We entered her home, and I helped this sweet soul down onto her knees. Then we began to pray. I poured out my soul to the Lord to let a sweet blessing of comfort come to her. About halfway through the prayer I felt a warmth and a peace come into my heart that I knew our prayers were being answered.

At the close of the prayer, I stood up and lifted her again from her knees. Peace radiated from her face. I held her hands for a moment and looked into her eyes. There was peace there.

Lawrence and I left. She came over and stood in the doorway as we went out and climbed into the car. Lawrence turned around and looked at her and then he said to me, "Dad, she sure was a sweet old grandma."

Well, there are many sweet old grandmas in the Church, and they love us and they need our love.

Some time ago I left a meeting of the Committee on Expenditures and went up to a local hospital to administer to a sweet little soul who had been there. As I finished, for some

29

reason I felt impressed to tell her, "I want you to know this hand shook hands with the prophet fifteen minutes ago." And she began to weep. Then a little lady across the room said, "Would you mind administering to me with that hand that shook hands with the prophet fifteen minutes ago?" And I administered to her, and then a lady in the bed next to her said, "Would you mind administering to me with that hand that shook hands with the prophet a few minutes ago?" And I administered to her.

Let us review the program, the Lord's program, for the care of our senior Saints.

First, the responsibility rests with the individual to do all he or she can to be a contributing member of society and of the Church, and give service to friends and children and loved ones. All these give soul satisfaction, which is so greatly needed. When health is sufficiently good, the Church provides many blessed opportunities for great service. The rich experience of these loved ones can be of such importance to the Church.

Many can accept calls as couples to fill full-time missions. Others may be called upon to officiate in the temples. Some may visit the temple regularly to do endowment work. Genealogical research is fascinating, stimulating, and fulfilling. Many can and should be called to teach Primary, Sunday School, and Relief Society. Our youth love mature Saints as teachers because they have time to care. Bishops may call the brethren to be home teachers and the sisters to do Relief Society visiting teaching.

Inasmuch as home teaching is never finished, many long-living men may help truly teach us by example what home teachers really should be. The Lord said, "He that loseth his life for my sake shall find it." (Matthew 10:39.) Our senior Saints may well be called upon to bake and cook or render compassionate service during funerals or other times of stress and need.

Second, the family should do all they can do. Those who

have mothers and fathers who are confined should care for them by furnishing such soul needs as love, care, and tenderness. You may recall the words of the epitaph:

> *Here lies David Elginbrod:*
> *Have mercy on him, God,*
> *As he would do if he were God*
> *And you were David Elginbrod.*

So we might also declare to you, try to understand them, try to anticipate their needs. Before you turn the financial responsibility of them over to the Church, state, or government, use every resource you or any member of your family has. Nursing home care provided by the Church was up 411 percent last year.

I believe the Savior would be pleased if we were to bring these souls back into our home, if possible, and if not, to pay the expenses from members of the family. I don't know of any mother or father in the Church who turned their children over to society during those prolonged sicknesses or during those first years of life when it took twenty-four hours a day to care for the infant child.

Third, after the individual and family have used all their resources, then the Church is called in to assist. Let me go back to one thought that came to me. I talked to a young man the other day, and he said that in his family a grandfather had been very critically ill and bedfast, and the family tended him during those long hours. The man had to wear a diaper, which the family changed regularly. Is that more than he would have done for them? No. We must not forget our family members.

Now to the Church. Welfare services reach into every life in the Church. We are interested in the physical health and emotional welfare of every member. Our beloved aged are a vital segment of the Church. They contribute more to our lives than we would dare to suppose.

For example, I have a sweet aunt, Beryl Hollindrake. She told me that when she was just three or four years old, my great-grandmother, her Grandmother Featherstone, would hold her on her lap and tell her about the Savior, all the beautiful stories. Then she recalled how my great-grandmother would tell her about the Savior's trial and how they beat him and cursed him and spit upon him—how they dragged him and forced him against the cross and drove huge spikes into his hands cruelly. She said, "As my grandmother would tell me these stories, tears would stream down her cheeks." And she said, "It was on the lap of my grandmother that I learned to love the Savior with all my heart and soul."

What a wonderful contribution our grandmothers and grandfathers can make if they will share some of the rich experiences and their testimonies with their children and grandchildren.

When I was stake president, we wanted the lonely, the heartsick, the despairing, even the inactive, young or old, to move into our stake so we would have a greater opportunity to serve. I have a great friend who, when he was called to be a stake president, canceled the high council Christmas party and had a special Christmas party for the senior Saints in the stake. And then on Christmas morning he called all the widows in his stake who had no one who cared.

Edgar A. Guest, in a great understanding of life, wrote many verses about home. Let me just extract a few from his poem on home:

> Ye've got t' weep t' make it home, ye've got t' sit an' sigh,
> An' watch beside a loved one's bed, an' know that
>   Death is nigh;
> An' in the stillness o' the night t' see Death's angel come.
> An' close the eyes o' her that smiled, an' leave her sweet
>   voice dumb.
> For these are scenes that grip the heart, an' when yer
>   tears are dried,

32

Ye find the home is dearer than it was, an' sanctified;
An' tuggin' at ye always are the pleasant memories
O' her that was an' is no more—ye can't escape from
these.

They may be pleasant memories, and they may not, depending on our care for them.

Stephen Horn, the president of California State University at Long Beach, said, "It is time we revised our concept of the 'old' to 'long-living' and accented not the declining powers of aging but the rising knowledge and experience that result from a long life."

Life can be so full and rich for our beloved senior Saints with snowy crowns. We love you and care for you. You make life so rich and meaningful for us. We pledge to be what we should be in our relationship to you. In James we read: "Pure religion and undefiled before God and the Father is this, To visit the fatherless and widows in their affliction." (James 1:27.)

"To visit the fatherless and widows in their affliction." It is my prayer that we may be filled with pure love of Christ toward our beloved senior Saints. This is his church. I believe if he were here he would spend much time with them. May we follow in his footsteps.

Chapter Six

The Blessing of a Mission

Charity is probably exemplified as much on a mission as any other dimension of life. We see wonderful, sweet Latter-day Saints who are committed and willing to sacrifice and pay all of their own expenses accept calls. They go wherever they are called and they serve seventy hours a week. They do the best job they can for the Lord.

Elder LeGrand Richards has been one of the great missionaries of the Church. I remember in a temple meeting he mentioned that he had been on four missions, had been a bishop and a stake president, had served as Presiding Bishop of the Church, and has served as an apostle for over twenty-five years. Then he said, "I have not withheld a particle of energy from the Lord. I have done as much as I possibly could in every single calling. After all these years I want everyone here to know that the Lord does not owe me one red cent."

We find true examples of love and compassion, the pure love of Christ, in the hearts of our missionaries—this wonderful army of committed Latter-day Saints who are criticized and ridiculed, who hunger and fast, who pray and plead, and who knock and plod steadily through city after city, village after village, from home to home, and occasionally find someone who will listen.

In modern-day revelation the Lord has told us, "And any man that shall go and preach this gospel of the kingdom, and fail not to continue faithful in all things, shall not be weary in mind, neither darkened, neither in body, limb, nor joint; and a hair of his head shall not fall to the ground unnoticed. And they shall not go hungry, neither athirst." (D&C 84:80.)

For two years our family served a mission in Texas. It was glorious and fulfilling beyond all expectations. When we first arrived Sister Featherstone went to the Lord and said, "We don't have much time. Please let me learn quickly so that the work will go forth." Later she said, "The Lord answered my prayers. He taught me several great lessons. One of those lessons came after the first three or four weeks in the mission field. When I was home I had been able to take about forty-five minutes in the afternoon to go out and curry down my Arabian horse. This way I would retreat into a world of my own for those few minutes. Now, in the mission field, I was unable to find the time, even a few minutes, for myself." She went to the Lord, knelt in prayer, and said, "Please, Heavenly Father, help me to find some time for myself while I am here." Then, just as clear as anything in this world, these words came into her mind: "My daughter, this is not your time. This is my time." We attempted to work with all our energy while we were on the Lord's time.

Let me share with you some of the faith experiences of the messengers with whom we served.

Elder and Sister Weidel wrote in their weekly letter: "Please, may we take a few moments to tell you of a spiritual experience this week. On Friday Elder Curtis, who was splitting with Elder Aloi, came to work with us and afterwards we took them home. Elder Aloi invited us in to see what a real elders' apartment looks like. He went through the back door to open the front door, and in a moment he came out beaming. 'Elder, come and see what has been brought to us,' he said. There on the table was a large supply of groceries. After a while Elder Curtis told us that Elder Aloi and his companion

35

had found a family that didn't have anything to eat, so they took all of their food out to them. My heart just about broke," wrote Sister Weidel. "The Lord does take care of his own."

One of the sweet and widowed sister missionaries, Sister Lorna Call Alder, said in her weekly letter to me: "The experiences of my mission have strengthened my testimony greatly. I cannot remember when I gained a testimony, but I do remember many experiences that have enriched and built upon the foundation I have. Of the many humbling experiences I've had, these past eight months have brought me closer to the Lord than at any period. I've lived through three revolutions in Mexico, which really built my testimony. Writing lessons for the Church brings one very close to the Lord, and he did bless me more than I can tell you. This mission has given me more twenty-four-hour spirituality than I have ever had. Other very spiritual uplifts in my life were times my sons were on their missions and they asked me to read the Book of Mormon while they were gone. My husband died while my oldest son was in Chile on his mission, and I was really humbled during that trying period. I am thankful for this experience of hard work and great blessings. With humility and thanksgiving, Sister Alder."

Another lovely couple was assigned to our mission, and before they arrived I received a letter from their daughter. In part she said, "You are getting two of the most wonderful folks in the world in a few weeks to serve in your mission for eighteen months. They are just tickled pink to be serving under you. They told me they plan to do whatever you tell them to do. You'll enjoy mom and dad. We'll miss them, so please take good care of them while they are there."

Most of our missionaries go into the field because they love the Lord Jesus Christ and they desire to serve him and bring souls unto him. There are a few who rationalize themselves out of a call or try to justify poor performance in the mission field—like the man who received his pay envelope and noticed that he had been shorted five dollars. He went to the paymaster and said, "You shorted me five dollars in my pay envelope this week." The paymaster responded, "Well, I have been expecting you. I noticed you didn't come in complaining last week when I overpaid you five dollars." The fellow said, "Well, I can tolerate one mistake, but not two in a row." Thousands of mature couples and widowed missionaries could be called if they would simply stop rationalizing why they shouldn't serve. Many of us understand the blessings that come when children and grandchildren kneel down at night and say, "Dear Heavenly Father, please bless grandma and grandpa, who are on a mission."

Sister Olsen mothered twelve children and supported all of her sons on missions. When she was called on a mission, they had the opportunity to support her.

I felt the love between missionaries and their families every day of my mission. Another fine young elder who was called on a mission had been driving cars across the country for a foreign car company. When his boss, who was not a member of the Church, heard he was going to be gone for two years to serve a mission, he said, "If you will stay home and work for me, I will give you a $28,000 Ferrari." Elder Granis completed his mission as a presiding zone leader.

Elder Daniel Gifford was promised in his patriarchal blessing that he would serve closely with a General Authority while he was on his mission. He wondered how this would be when he received his mission call to Texas, where the mission president had only served two or three months. While he was in the Missionary Training Center listening to the final session of October general conference, he heard President Tanner announce the next speaker would be Elder Vaughn J. Featherstone, a member of the First Quorum of the Seventy and newly called president of the Texas San Antonio Mission. When Elder Gifford was later called to be an assistant to the mission president, he shared his patriarchal blessing promise with us. Do you think he has any question about whose work this is?

One elder who was transferred from another mission

37

wanted to go home. He knew his parents wanted him to stay and complete his mission. In one of the many interviews we had, he said that five previous elders in his ward had abandoned their missions and returned home early. I thought what a great disservice the first elder did to the other young men who followed his poor example. I made a solemn vow that this elder would not go home until his mission was completed successfully. Every week for thirteen to fifteen weeks he would write in his letter to the president all the reasons he should be released from his mission. Each week I wrote a letter or response.

After all these weeks, I received a letter that appeared the same as the others—until I got to the P.S. He said, "President, you are winning, and you know it." I sat in my office and tears filled my eyes.

Vince Lombardi, the great football coach, said, "The harder you fight for something, the harder it is to surrender." This elder completed his mission as a presiding zone leader. He had great warmth and a great talent to teach; he loves and cares for people; and he is extremely spiritual. He returned home with an honorable release from a very successful mission, married a beautiful girl in the temple, and now they live near the temple, which they visit regularly. He set a fine example for all prospective missionaries in his ward.

Elder Sheffield had been under the knife eleven times in major surgery and many more times in minor surgery. The greatest desire of his life was that the surgery would make him acceptable for a mission. A year before he entered the mission field he had his final operation. On his mission he averaged seventy hours a week in proselyting. He was greatly loved by all, and a great blessing to missionaries who thought they had problems. In one interview his companion told me that Elder Sheffield's shoulder would separate and fall out of place quite often. When this happened he was in severe pain. It seemed to happen most often during the night. When I interviewed Elder Sheffield I suggested that we put him in a local hospital and have the doctors do what needed to be done to correct this problem. He looked me in the eye and, with a sternness seldom seen, said, "President, I have spent much of my life in hospitals, and when I complete my mission I am returning to several more major surgical operations. I promised the Lord that if he would let me serve a mission, I would not spend one day in the hospital during the two years no matter how sick I was or how much I suffered."

What are the blessings of a mission? Can ye tell? (See Alma 26:2.) Maybe Brother and Sister William Keith Clark can.

"Dear President Featherstone," they wrote, "we were happy to receive your nice letter. I'm sure we love you already." (Bless them, they didn't even know me and yet they could love me.) They continued: "We are not too young anymore. William Keith Clark is eighty-one years old. He has been a bishop's counselor, a bishop, and a patriarch for thirty-one years. I, Ellen Clark, am seventy-six years of age. I have been a music director and a teacher in all the organizations of the Church, ward and stake. We have had an abundant life and love to teach the gospel. We have ten children, all married in the temple and working in the Church. We had our reunion recently—56 grandchildren and 26 great-grandchildren! This is four missions for my husband and three for me. Our happiest moments are teaching the gospel of Jesus Christ."

Every missionary is a story of love and sacrifice. I love each of them so much. Their great devotion to the cause, their love of the Lord, and their willingness to serve him whose work this is will bless their lives and their posterity forever. You see, my beloved brothers and sisters, every soul should have the privilege of hearing about the restoration of the gospel of Jesus Christ. Those who respond to the call shall "not be weary in mind, neither darkened, neither in body, limb, nor joint; and a hair of [their] head[s] shall not fall to the ground unnoticed. And they shall not go hungry, neither athirst." (D&C 84:80.) We must seek out every soul and do it with the pure love of Christ.

We must not judge the people. We do not know whom

God has prepared, but we do know, as the Prophet Joseph Smith has stated: "The Standard of Truth has been erected; no unhallowed hand can stop the work from progressing; persecutions may rage, mobs may combine, armies may assemble, calumny may defame, but the truth of God will go forth boldly, nobly, and independent, until it has penetrated every continent, visited every clime, swept every country, and sounded in every ear, till the purposes of God shall be accomplished, and the great Jehovah shall say the work is done." (*History of the Church* 4:540.)

God bless us that all who may be able to serve will make themselves available for a mission call.

Chapter Seven

"My Sheep Hear My Voice"

The Prophet Joseph Smith once stated, "A man filled with the love of God is not content with blessing his family alone, but ranges through the whole world, anxious to bless the whole human race." (*History of the Church* 4:227.)

Missionaries of the Church of Jesus Christ have unparalleled opportunities for practicing true charity, as they serve their Heavenly Father and share with their fellowmen the blessings of the gospel. My family and I had the opportunity of serving in the Texas San Antonio Mission, and there we saw every day the fruits of the missionaries' efforts—and the blessings that come to missionaries themselves as they immerse themselves in service to others and to the Lord. During those years we witnessed on innumerable occasions outpourings of the Spirit of the Lord upon people. The Savior said, "My sheep hear my voice." (John 10:27.) I bear testimony to that statement of fact. The sheep do indeed hear the voice of the Shepherd. May I share with you some of our experiences and observations.

The Savior said, "He that findeth his life shall lose it; and he that loseth his life for my sake shall find it." (Matthew 10:39.) And during his visit to the inhabitants of the American continent, he said, "Blessed are the poor in spirit who come

41

unto me, for theirs is the kingdom of heaven." (3 Nephi 12:3.)

One way in which missionaries exhibit charity is in learning self-denial—in losing themselves as they labor for the Church and kingdom of God.

One elder in our mission had some pretty serious health problems. He had a skin allergy, bronchial and sinus problems, and other physical ailments. When I arrived in the mission, he was sleeping in for fear of catching the flu. After lunch he would sleep for a couple of hours, again to keep from catching a cold or the flu. His companion was frustrated and called me. I called the elder's doctor, and he told me, "Well, his condition is bad, but it's better than it was when he came into the mission field. It's not going to change much no matter how many hours he works."

Then I visited with the elder in my office. I suggested that I would rather see him sick with the flu legitimately than always worrying about it. I discussed with him the principle of suffering in silence, of simply going to work and doing what the Lord had called him to do. I said, "The doctor says your condition isn't going to change no matter how much or how little you do. We've done and are doing all we can do—so why don't you learn to suffer in silence?"

Bless his heart, he took the counsel and put it into practice. He became one of the top missionaries in the mission. Within about six weeks he had been made a training senior companion, then a district leader. What a great missionary he became! He discovered how to suffer in silence and do the work. He was a great example of self-denial.

Another missionary had a bad back and was in constant pain. He did not know that I knew of his condition. He loved missionary work so much he kept his condition a secret for fear he might be released from his mission. Another elder had ruined both knees in sports competition. His knees were being held together by cartilage. He asked for a blessing from the mission president who preceded me, and was able to endure another full year, though every step he took gave him great pain. When I interviewed him prior to his release, he pleaded with me to let him remain on his mission two more years.

An elder from Florida once asked me, "What is the mission record for pure proselyting hours?" I told him, "I understand it is 104 hours." Within two weeks he and his companion sent in their report of 108 hours. Now he had to violate some rules to do that, but how can one be critical of an elder with the heart of a champion? A choice friend of mine once said, "The coward never starts; the weak die on the way; only the strong come through." This missionary was one of the strongest.

The mission life is not easy. It requires self-denial, mental and physical exertion, maturity, self-mastery, spirituality, and a very strong, positive mental attitude. It requires an elder to be a man and not a boy. A mission should be a spartan life; it requires resiliency and total commitment.

To those who are preparing for missions, I would like to say that it is not one of the most glorious experiences of a lifetime because it is easy; the rewards do not come from the glamour of the call or the personal attention and accolades that members extend to you after you receive the call. Missions are not fulfilling because of assignments to exotic places. The fulfillment comes to the missionary who is willing to practice self-denial. The reward comes from Him in whose service we have been enlisted. No other reward or compensation can compare to the wage received from the Lord of the vineyard.

Self-denial may take form in many different ways. It may mean delaying an education or marriage. It usually requires a commitment to study the scriptures and discussions instead of watching television or movies. It requires saving money for a mission instead of spending it on dates, clothes, cars, and other forms of personal gratification. A young man or woman who spends a dollar a day on hamburgers, ice cream, or other personal indulgences spends thirty dollars a month that could be saved toward a mission.

Self-indulgence—the opposite of self-denial—is addictive

in all its forms, just as drugs, nicotine, alcohol, and reading pornography are addictive. Gambling, watching television to excess, overeating, oversleeping, uncontrolled thinking, lusting, swearing, telling dirty or lewd jokes, dressing immodestly, lying, cheating, playing cards—all are addictive. If you think not, try to change. You will have strong withdrawal pains. Conversely, the life of self-denial builds strength of character, integrity, health, self-control, confidence, and self-respect.

The youth of today are exposed to two great extremes. The world is polarizing—and the poles are oceans apart. Our youth are not seeking the easy life. It isn't the glamour of exotic places that appeals to young people who go on missions. It is the life of service to fellowman, the desire to become increasingly spiritual, the quest for purity of heart. It is engaging in the cause of the Master. The desire to be involved is a cause that demands total commitment of soul and mind.

One missionary who served a mission in Buenos Aires, Argentina, caught the vision of total selfless service and self-denial. He wrote to me:

"Six months before I left my mission you spoke at our mission conference in Buenos Aires. I felt the Spirit resting upon me so strongly that afterwards I felt a voice inside me tell me to seek a promise from you. I struggled forward and said to you, 'Can you look me in the eye and promise me that I can baptize ten people before I complete my mission?' I don't even know if those were my exact words, but they expressed the desire I had. You see, I had not baptized even a single soul, and my mission was soon to be over. You looked me in the eye and promised with a voice of certainty that should I be faithful to the utmost, with all my heart, might, mind, and strength, I would baptize ten people. In my heart I knew that you could not be lying, and I knew that I had received the promise I sought.

"I worked with all my heart and with all my might and mind and strength, and my mission ended following two years of faithful endeavoring. The Lord did bless me, and the promise was fulfilled. Whereas for nearly two years I had baptized no one, the last Saturday of my mission my companion and I entered the waters and opened the doors of God's kingdom for fifteen beautiful and repentant children of our Father in heaven."

Elder Mortenson had caught the vision of total selfless service and self-denial, and he achieved his goal. One who truly has involved the principle of self-denial in his or her life finds that it brings more joy and satisfaction than the accumulation of a fortune.

How blessed are those who learn the lessons of self-denial and who give great service to the Master in the missions of the Church. And how blessed are those who listen to the promptings of the Spirit and accept the message of salvation brought to them by these selfless messengers.

One such person was Brother Guttierrez, a strong man of integrity and character. I met him one Sunday when I was attending church in McAllen, Texas. One of our missionaries introduced me to the Guttierrez family: father, mother, and four adult children, all fine, upstanding citizens of that community. I bore testimony to the family after we had been introduced. Then I put my arms around the shoulders of Brother Guttierrez and told him that the time would come when he, his wife, and their four sons and daughters would be sealed together in one of the Lord's temples by one who was authorized and held these sealing powers. After I left the family, one of the elders came over to me and told me that three of the family were being baptized that day, and he told me who they were. The mother and father were not among the three. I counseled briefly with the elder and then left to go to Bishop Joseph Parker's home for dinner.

As we arrived at Bishop Parker's home, I had a strong impression to go back to the chapel and talk with Mr. Guttierrez. I excused myself and drove approximately ten miles back to the chapel to talk with Brother Guttierrez. When I arrived at the chapel, he was standing outside alone. I sat down with him on a bench outside the chapel and we talked. He said, "This is a beautiful chapel. The Church is very wealthy. I need to prepare myself so I can afford to join."

I said, "Do you believe Joseph Smith was a prophet?"

"Yes, I do."

"Do you believe the Book of Mormon is true?"

"I believe the Book of Mormon is true."

I asked him, "Why aren't you being baptized?"

He stood up, raised his arm in the air, and said, "This is a magnificent church. I have got to find another job so I can afford to belong."

I then said to him, "The promise in Malachi about paying our tithes and offerings is true. I know that the Lord is not interested in the amount of the offering, but rather in the intent of the heart. Tithing, or ten percent, of fifteen dollars is a greater contribution than five percent or seven percent of a hundred thousand dollars. The Church members who pay tithes and offerings, however great or small, receive the promised blessings." I told him of a young man I knew who had to wear to church the kind of shoes nurses wear, since he had no other shoes that would fit him. I told of people who struggled financially to pay tithing when they couldn't afford rent or clothes. Then I testified to him that the God I worship, the great God of heaven, would pour out blessings he could not contain if he would be baptized and keep the commandments. This sweet Lamanite brother, concerned that he couldn't afford to be a member of Christ's true church, indeed could never afford *not* to be a member.

One day two of our zone leaders called me on the phone. They wanted me to come out to a small community in Texas. They had been teaching a former Lutheran minister, a Mr. Joens, and his family. Mr. Joens had moved to Knippa, Texas, where he was raising a few cattle and had several beehives and a garden. The elders asked me if I would come, I said yes, and we set a date. Then they contacted Brother Joens to see if it was all right with him. They suggested to him that I might answer some of his questions concerning the Church.

We drove down a long dirt road through his property until we came to the Joens home. Mr. Joens and his wife and baby were there. The other children were in school. After they welcomed us in, I explained a little about my calling and then asked if he had any questions that I might answer for him. He said he couldn't think of any. So we visited for a while, and I suggested some questions that the elders had said might be of concern to him. I answered those questions. Then I asked again if our discussion had raised any questions in his mind. Again he said no. We repeated the aforementioned process a second and a third time by way of discussion of questions that were often raised.

After about an hour of spiritual discussion I asked if we could kneel and have a prayer in his home. I said, "I feel impressed to leave a prayer and blessing in your home. As the head of the house, would you feel all right about that?" He said yes. At the conclusion of the prayer, as we stood up, he said, "About two weeks ago the elders and our family knelt down to pray and asked the Lord to help us find out if the Church was true, if Joseph Smith truly was a prophet, and if the Book of Mormon was a second witness for Christ. During the prayer, I was told that before I would be baptized the 'president' would come to my home and offer a prayer and a blessing." He was baptized the following week in a beautiful river that flows through his property. What a great strength he and his family are to the Uvalde Ward!

When we took one of our missionaries, Elder Gibson, to the airport prior to his departure from the mission, Sister Hilscher and her son were also there. As we walked down the concourse to the departure gate she said, "Have you ever heard my story?" I told her that I had not. Then she related to me the story of her conversion.

Sister Hilscher loves people and loves to visit with them. Her mobility has been impaired for many years, and she gets around on crutches. When the elders knocked on her door she invited them in. She visited with them and they persuaded her to listen to the discussions. After the third discussion she said she could see they were planning to baptize her. She told them, "When I was a little girl I had a great desire to join the Roman Catholic Church. The desire intensified as I grew older. I went to my mother early in my teens to see if she would grant me the privilege of being baptized a Catholic." Her mother told her, "Absolutely not. I will not permit it until you turn eighteen; then you can make your own decision." When she turned eighteen, she was immediately baptized into the Catholic Church. Then she turned to Elder Gibson and said, "All of my life I had wanted to be a Catholic, and since turning eighteen many years ago, I have been. I am a Catholic now, and I will continue to be a Catholic as long as I live." Then she told me, "Suddenly, clear as anything I have ever heard, a voice said to me, 'But what do you know about it?'" She recalled, "I turned back to the elders and said, 'But after all, elders, what do I know about it?'" She was baptized with her teenage son, and they are very active in the Church.

At the same time Sister Hilscher told me her story, Brother Jackson and his wife were also at the airport to see Elder Gibson off. As the final boarding was called, Elder Gibson embraced Brother Jackson, who said to him, "Remember the night I told you never to come back again?" Elder Gibson quietly said, "Yes, I remember." "Thank God you came back," Brother Jackson said with tears in his eyes. At a solemn assembly in San Antonio, Texas, along with Brother Joens, the former Lutheran minister, was Brother Jackson, both seated on the front row, both elders quorum presidents, both prepared to pass the sacrament at the first solemn assembly ever held in San Antonio.

The Lord has prepared marvelous people like Sister Hilscher and Brother Jackson and his family. What blessings they are to the Church!

At Bryan, Texas, I was invited to speak to a group of

Young Adults. I spoke for about an hour, focusing on a theme of temple marriage and quoting several of President Spencer W. Kimball's statements regarding the temple. At the conclusion of my talk the time was turned over to the group for a special testimony meeting. One of the sweet Young Adults, about twenty years of age, stood up and said, in essence, "I have been a member of the Church only a short time. The saddest day of my parents' lives was the day I joined the Church. My father is a Baptist minister, and he and mother felt I was lost forever. The one hope my father clung to tenaciously was that when I got married he would be able to perform the ceremony for me. After hearing President Featherstone speak this morning and after listening to the statements from our prophet, President Kimball, now I know that not only will my father not perform the ceremony, but he will not even be able to see me married, for I am going to follow our prophet's counsel and be married in the temple. What use is it to have a prophet if we do not follow his counsel?" Such maturity of thought for one so young in the Church!

A wonderful family in Corpus Christi who were Baptist and very active were tracted out by the missionairies. They listened to the message and believed it, but said they were tempted by all kinds of thoughts. What would the members of the Baptist congregation think? What would their neighbors think? What would the people they worked with think? What about all the false things they had heard about our Church? They had believed these things, and now they had discovered they were not true. However, their neighbors, co-workers, and friends didn't know they weren't true. This wonderful family became less and less active in the Baptist church. Soon they were not attending at all. About a year later the father decided they should get active in church, so they went to the chapel of The Church of Jesus Christ of Latter-day Saints. I attended their baptism. Now the father and two sons are priesthood bearers.

49

Another man had committed a major crime against society. While in prison, although he had never heard of the Church, he came across a copy of the Book of Mormon and believed it. When he was released from prison he got married, and when their first son came along he named him Mormon. Later the missionaries came to his home, and now the family members are part of Jesus Christ's true church.

Two of our elders were teaching a family, discussing the First Vision and the need for modern apostles and prophets. The family was progressing and all attended church except the father, who had stayed home to mow the lawn and work in the yard. Then one day, in the middle of fast and testimony meeting, in came the father to join his family. He said that while he was mowing the lawn he had felt an overwhelming impression from the Spirit that told him he should be in church with his family. He stood up in fast and testimony meeting and bore a powerful witness that he knew the Church was true and he desired to be baptized. This sweet family is now active in the Church.

William Ernest Henley, wracked with pain and torment, his broken body emaciated and worn out, composed the monumental work "Invictus":

> *Out of the night that covers me*
> *Black as the Pit from pole to pole*
> *I thank whatever gods may be*
> *For my unconquerable soul.*
>
> *In the fell clutch of circumstance*
> *I have not winced nor cried aloud.*
> *Under the bludgeonings of chance*
> *My head is bloody, but unbowed.*
>
> *Beyond this place of wrath and tears*
> *Looms but the Horror of the shade,*
> *And yet the menace of the years*
> *Finds and shall find me unafraid.*

It matters not how strait the gate,
How charged with punishments the scroll,
I am the master of my fate:
I am the captain of my soul.

We are each the captain of our own soul, and we each determine our own fate. I know with all my heart and soul that self-denial and selfless service can bring great blessings to those who follow the way of the Master and who heed the promptings of his Spirit. May the Lord bless our wonderful, devoted missionaries and those who have listened to their message and entered God's kingdom through the waters of baptism!

Chapter Eight

The Impact Teacher

Sometimes acts of charity—or, more accurately, the pure love of Christ—take years to mature into fruition. Such is the case with great teachers, the hosts of workers who train and teach and who are indeed impact teachers.

President David O. McKay said, "There is no greater responsibility in the world than the training of a human soul." A great part of the personal stewardship of every parent and teacher in the Church is to teach and train. How well we fill this divinely commissioned task may well have eternal implications for many.

One of America's philosophers, John Dewey, said, "The deepest urge in human nature is the desire to be important. It is a gnawing, unfaltering hunger. People sometimes become invalids in order to win sympathy and to get a feeling of importance. Some authorities declare that people may actually go insane in order to find, in that dreamland of insanity, the feeling of importance that has been denied them in the harsh world of reality."

What miracles an impact teacher can achieve by giving honest appreciation and a sense of self-worth! The parent or teacher who honestly satisfies this heart hunger will hold a child or a class in the palm of his hand.

Some years ago when Aldin Porter was president of the Boise North Stake, he dropped by the home of Glen Clayton, who was the Scoutmaster in his ward. Glen and his son were working together repairing a bicycle. President Porter stood and talked to them for a few minutes and then left. Several hours later he returned and the father and son were still working on the bike together. President Porter said, "Glen, with the wages you make per hour you could have bought a new bike, considering the time you have spent repairing this old one."

Glen stood up and said, "I'm not repairing a bike, I'm training a boy!"

That year twenty-one boys achieved the rank of Eagle Scout in Glen's troop. Impact teachers do not teach lessons, they teach souls.

Remembering why educators fail, someone furnished a rhyming explanation:

> *College professor says:*
> *Such rawness in a pupil is a shame;*
> *High school preparation is to blame.*
>
> *High school teacher says:*
> *Good heavens, what crudity—the boy's a fool.*
> *The fault of course is the grammar school.*
>
> *Grade school teacher cries:*
> *From such stupidity may I be spared;*
> *They send them to me so unprepared.*
>
> *Kindergarten teacher says:*
> *Such lack of training did I never see—*
> *What kind of woman must the mother be?*
>
> *Mother laments:*
> *Poor helpless child—he is not to blame,*
> *His father's folks are just the same.*

Recently, after a priesthood leadership meeting at a stake

conference where I spoke about a father's role with his family, a man came up and introduced himself. He said he was going to write to me, and a few days later I received this letter. I quote only part:

"Dear Bishop Featherstone:

"You possibly don't recall the brief conversation we had on the stand at the stake conference last Saturday night. I told you I have a seventeen-year-old son to whom I hadn't spoken a kind word in nine years and I was going home and tell him how much I loved him.

"He has caused his mother and me many hours of heartbreak, especially in the last two years. He and I haven't had a father-son relationship in over half his life. Isn't that a frightening thought? However, the little unhappiness he has caused us is nothing compared to the lonely hours he must have spent because of me all those years. The many nights he went to bed feeling so unloved and unwanted by me, his father!"

In Ezekiel we read about the ancient proverb that the fathers have eaten sour grapes and it hath set the children's teeth on edge. (See Ezekiel 18.2.) Paraphrasing President Harold B. Lee's statement, "The greatest teaching we will ever do is within the walls of our own home." We have a sacred trust to teach our children the principles of truth; but equally important is to love and care in following the way of the Master.

Impact teachers are not cast in a certain mold in the spirit world and introduced on earth's scene at just the proper time. Every leader in the kingdom can become an impact teacher. A teacher's notoriety may not reach much past the quorum or class, but his influence may be felt in the eternities.

We sometimes get our priorities all mixed up, as stated by a national columnist, Erma Bombeck, in her column titled "Mike Will Come Back, Won't He?"

When Mike was three he wanted a sandbox, and his father said, "There goes the yard. We'll have kids over here day and night and they'll throw sand and it'll kill the grass for sure."

And Mike's mother said, "It'll come back."

When Mike was five, he wanted a jungle gym with swings that would take his breath away and bars to take him to the summit. And his father said, "Good grief, I've seen those things in back yards, and do you know what the yards look like? Mud holes in a pasture! Kids digging their gym shoes in the ground. "It'll kill the grass."

And Mike's mother said, "It'll come back."

Between breaths, when Daddy was blowing up the plastic swimming pool, he warned, "They'll track water everywhere and they'll have a million water fights and you won't be able to take out the garbage without stepping in mud up to your neck and we'll have the only brown lawn on the block."

And Mike's mother said, "It'll come back."

When Mike was twelve, he volunteered his yard for a camp-out. As the boys hoisted the tents and drove in the spikes, Mike's father said, "You know those tents and all those big feet are going to trample down every single blade of grass, don't you? Don't bother to answer. I know what you're going to say—It'll come back."

Just when it looked as if the new seed might take root, winter came and the sled runners beat it into ridges. And Mike's father shook his head and said, "I never asked for much in this life—only a patch of grass."

And Mike's mother said, "It'll come back."

Now Mike is eighteen. The lawn this year is beautiful—green and alive and rolling out like a carpet along the drive where gym shoes had trod; along the garage where bicycles used to fall; and around the flower beds where little boys used to dig with teaspoons.

But Mike's father doesn't notice. He looks anxiously beyond the yard and asks, "Mike will come back, won't he?"

The impact teacher cares with an attitude of pure charity. The impact teacher asks, "What would the Savior do when faced with this problem?"

In 1966 President Spencer W. Kimball addressed the seminary and institute teachers and supervisors. He titled his talk "What I Hope You Will Teach My Grandchildren." His talk was filled with profound truths. Every teacher in the Church should read and apply it:

"So I salute you, the trainers and inspirers of youth. Your responsibility is awesome. Your opportunities to become saviors are near limitless. We do not excuse the parents in their failures, but we must place the burden upon your strong backs to carry on. It must be brilliant and effective. . . .

"I'm depending on you to teach my offspring. I have twenty-six grandchildren. One died an infant and went to the Celestial Kingdom. Two are married and finished with their conventional schooling. But we still have twenty-three to be taught by you. . . . Now you can see why I'm so concerned about the men who will be employed . . . and why I hope they will be men of valor and faith, of forcefulness and courage, and of example. However, I expect nothing more for my own than for the other multitudes of Latter-day Saint youth."

Then in conclusion he said, "What do I wish you to teach my grandchildren and all others? Above all, I hope you will teach them faith in the living God and in his Only Begotten Son—not a superficial, intellectual kind of acceptance, but a deep spiritual inner feeling of dependence and closeness. . . . I hope that you will teach righteousness, pure and undefiled. I hope that if any of God's children are out in spiritual darkness, you will come to them with a lamp and light their way; if they are out in the cold of spiritual bleakness with its frigidity penetrating their bones, you will come to them holding their hands a little way, you will walk miles and miles with them lifting them, strengthening them, encouraging them and inspiring them."

Yes, we must teach truths of the gospel to our youth with that kind of conviction.

An impact teacher will be pure. President Kimball said, at a Regional Representatives seminar, "It takes a clean fountain to send forth pure and clear water."

The work of the impact teacher is primarily—and with greatest and lasting emphasis—to save the soul of the student. If we do all else and lose the boy or girl, we have failed in our sacred and holy stewardship. Let us declare as Job: "Oh that my words were now written! oh that they were printed in a book! That they were graven with an iron pen and lead in the rock for ever!" (Job 19:23-24.)

The work of the impact teacher is to save every soul in the class or quorum!

56

Dr. Gustav Eckstein, one of the world's renowned ornithologists, worked in the same laboratory for over twenty-five years. He bred and crossbred species of birds, and kept meticulous records on the varieties and hybrids of birds in his laboratory. Each day when he would enter his laboratory he would go down two or three stairs to the stereo. He would put on classical music and turn the volume up very loud. Then he would go about his work. The birds would sing along with the classical music. At the end of the day, about 5:30 P.M., he would turn off the stereo and leave for home.

After twenty-five years he had to hire a new custodian. One evening after Dr. Eckstein left the laboratory, the new custodian thought the place should be aired out, so he opened all the windows. The next morning when Dr. Eckstein went into his laboratory he saw the open windows and noted that every bird had flown out during the night. He was devastated, his life's work ruined. By habit or instinct, he went to the stereo and turned the classical music up very loud. Then he sat down on the steps, put his head in his hands, and wept.

The strains of music carried out through the open windows, through the trees, and down the streets. In a few moments Dr. Eckstein heard the fluttering of wings. He looked up and saw that the birds were beginnning to come back into the laboratory through the open windows. "And," he reported, "every bird came back!"

Our youth will hear the classical music of the gospel, and if they have an impact teacher, every boy and girl will come back. God bless the parents, bishops, and leaders of youth, seminary and institute teachers, and Sunday School teachers who have been raised up for this special time with a special mission as impact teachers to this great generation.

Chapter Nine

The House of the Lord

We oftentimes do not think about the temple as a place where charitable acts are performed. But just the thought of going to a temple and there doing work for our kindred dead, many of whom we have never seen, and with little knowledge or understanding, but giving to a soul the opportunity to accept or reject the vicarious work done there—this truly is one of the most Christlike acts of charity that can be performed.

The home may become the second most sacred place on the earth. Holy temples are houses of the Lord. They are built as "Holiness to the Lord" edifices wherein worthy members of the Church may perform ordinances. All who have entered these sacred sanctuaries come away from them with a greater spirit, with deeper love for Him whose work this is, and with a profound sense of gratitude for knowledge of things that reach far into eternity.

Each temple is adorned with intricate and ornate woodwork. The most skilled craftsmen are invited to add to, mend, or refurbish these holy houses. No inferior work is ever acceptable. The painters, carpenters, plumbers, electricians, and other skilled artisans seem to be caught up in the vision that truly, in the house of the Lord only the best work should be done. Everyone senses and feels a need to perform at a level of excellence unmatched elsewhere.

I have recently paused to note the beautiful woodwork in many temple rooms. Detail and design are intricate and the work is flawless. Painting is done with such care that it seems near perfect.

Escape with me for a few moments and let us visit the celestial room in the Salt Lake Temple. You are seated in a beautiful, high-back, overstuffed chair. Each piece of furniture elegantly complements all else in the room. The room is basically white, with furniture, chandeliers, lamps, sculptures, and woodwork bringing subdued color and aesthetic balance. Subdued lighting provides a warm, comfortable atmosphere. The beautiful carpet lends additional elegance to the room. Beautiful pieces of artwork are displayed on pedestals and tables. There is a quiet, yea, more than quiet, a holy hush that seems omnipresent. Beautiful archlike doors lead to three sealing rooms, the middle door leading to the sacred Holy of Holies. One is filled with awe and deep spiritual contemplation as his or her gaze turns toward these three rooms, beautifully decorated in magnificent simplicity. The Holy of Holies door is closed, but our minds and spirits oftentimes enter for a moment, realizing that there is the most sacred of all rooms. The words of Moses echo in our minds: "Put off thy shoes from off thy feet, for the place whereon thou standest is holy ground." (Exodus 3:5.)

In our mind's eye we may see our beloved prophet, dressed in white, kneeling at the beautiful altar. We may even venture to imagine the words of a prayer. "And do thou, O God, open the doors of all nations that thy servants may spread forth the glorious gospel of thy Son. Let thy Spirit lead thy servants whithersoever thou listeth to take them. And also, Almighty Father, multiply the number of the messengers by double, yea, even four and ten fold. Cause that this people, the little flock whom thou lovest, will put on their beautiful garments and labor with pure and Christlike love. We realize the hour is nigh upon us when, as the prophets foretold, the signs of the coming

59

of the Son of Man will take place. Father, please give us more laborers for the vineyard. Give us time that we may penetrate every heart of every soul that walks the earth. It consumes us to consider that one soul should be lost.

"O Father, bless us that we will come to a knowledge and an understanding of the magnificent love of Jesus Christ, thine Only Begotten Son. Our souls are humbled to the dust of the earth as we consider the great atonement that was wrought for us by thy Beloved Son. Bless us with a portion of his love and his compassion. In our state of nothingness we acknowledge him as our Lord of lords, our King of kings, the great I Am, the God of modern Israel. Bless us that we will not withhold a particle of energy as we serve.

"Guide this thy servant, whom thou hast called to a position. I did not seek—and, in fact, prayed that it would not take place—to lead this people. I love thee, Holy Father. My life is committed to the work which thou hast called me to do. Thou couldst not ask me to do anything I would not do. My soul is filled with love even to the consuming of my flesh. The thought of harming one of the tiniest of thy creations is abhorrent to my soul. Take me, Lord, into thy bosom; mold my soul as clay in thine hands. I am thine. I will do all I am commanded to do in faith, love, service, and deed."

In a few moments we see our beloved prophet emerge from the Holy of Holies, an aura of light surrounding him, his countenance white and pure, and we know that God must love him more than word can express or heart can feel.

We once again feel impressed with the moment in the celestial room when time seems to stop and the cares of the world vanish away.

There are places too beautiful to describe. Not only is it aesthetically beautiful, but it is a spiritual haven. Those who have been here return over and over again in their minds, a moment of escape and quiet solitude in the silent chambers of the mind.

To the youth, may I encourage you to prepare yourselves that these things I have described might become a reality in your lives. All the money in the world cannot buy entrance into the Lord's holy house, and yet the most destitute Saint who is worthy may find refuge and haven there. If we could see into eternity and have opened to our view the significance and absolute essentiality of temple ordinances, we would never cease to labor to gain worthy entrance.

The prophet Amulek says, "Do not procrastinate the day of your repentance until the end; for after this day of life, which is given us to prepare for eternity, behold, if we do not improve our time while in this life, then cometh the night of darkness wherein there can be no labor performed.

"Ye cannot say, when you are brought to that awful crisis, that I will repent, that I will return to my God. Nay, ye cannot say this; for that same spirit which doth possess your bodies at the time that ye go out of this life, that same spirit will have power to possess your body in that eternal world." (Alma 34:33-34.)

These words seem to have a tone of love and pleading, as do the Savior's words in the Doctrine and Covenants: "Therefore I command you to repent—repent, lest I smite you by the rod of my mouth, and by my wrath, and by my anger, and your sufferings be sore—how sore you know not, how exquisite you know not, yea, how hard to bear you know not.

"For behold, I, God, have suffered these things for all, that they might not suffer if they would repent;

"But if they would not repent they must suffer even as I;

"Which suffering caused myself, even God, the greatest of all, to tremble because of pain, and to bleed at every pore, and to suffer both body and spirit—and would that I might not drink the bitter cup, and shrink—

"Nevertheless, glory be to the Father, and I partook and finished my preparations unto the children of men.

"Wherefore, I command you again to repent, lest I humble you with my almighty power. . . ." (D&C 19:15-20.)

In his great love he has called us to repent that we might have the burden of transgression lifted from our souls. In his all-loving way he said, "Learn of me, and listen to my words; walk in the meekness of my Spirit, and you shall have peace in me." (D&C 19:23.)

In doing his will we find life, and that more abundantly. Let us prepare ourselves to go to the temple. Let us submit ourselves to the living Christ and drink from the pure fountain of living waters.

"O that I were an angel, and could have the wish of mine heart, that I might go forth and speak with the trump of God, with a voice to shake the earth, and cry repentance unto every people!

"Yea, I would declare unto every soul, as with the voice of thunder, repentance and the plan of redemption, that they should repent and come unto our God, that there might not be more sorrow upon all the face of the earth.

"But behold, I am a man, and do sin in my wish; for I ought to be content with the things which the Lord hath allotted unto me." (Alma 29:1-3.)

We cannot be content until we have done all in our power to persuade every soul to partake more fully.

Temples are built unto the Lord. They are built as perfect as man can create them. Several years ago I had the privilege of traveling on Church business with Elder and Sister Thomas S. Monson. While we were in Hamilton, New Zealand, Elder Monson inspected the temple. As we visited each impressive room, there was little that needed to be improved. Finally, we came to a large glass door approximately four feet wide, eight feet tall, and one inch thick. It cost several hundred dollars. There was a tiny crack several inches long in the beautiful door. It was not very noticeable unless someone pointed it out, which the temple president did. He said, "This is a costly door. I have been trying to decide whether to replace it or to wait until it gets worse." He said that a new door would have to be ordered from England and would be very expensive. Without any hesitation, Elder Monson said, "Replace it. This is the Lord's holy house, and it must be perfect."

Can we do anything less than our best? Can we build anything less than the best? Can we be anything less than our very best selves in order to pay appropriate homage and adoration to our Savior?

Yes, my beloved brothers and sisters, there are temples where an enlightened people of God may go. His Spirit is there because he has visited there. Peace abounds, love overflows, light and intelligence permeate every teaching. Burdens are relieved. Visit the temples of the Most High God; escape from the cares of the world. Sit down in the celestial room and let his Spirit enshroud you with his love. He lives and he loves us. We live and we love him. We are wont to follow in his steps and be in his presence.

May we inspire every youth and young adult, every prospective elder, and every honest-in-heart nonmember to subscribe to his teachings and one day go to his holy house. Prepare, and then "come and see." It is a house of peace, a house of wisdom, a house of purity, a house of God.

Chapter Ten

Time Limits

Time is measured to man only, and it seems to many of us when we go through the deep struggles of life that time has passed and our time limits have run out. But charity is constant—it has no time limit. We must simply put our trust in the Lord and wait until in his time we are removed from the tests and trials of life. Charity also calls for great reflection on our part as to how best to use the time allotted to us to fulfill the measure of our creation.

Some years ago I remember watching a television movie in which a U.S military man who was a prisoner of war during the Korean War was being tried in a military court. As the movie progressed it appeared to me that the man was unquestionably guilty of treason. He had given the enemy secrets and information that he should have guarded with his life, and the prosecution proved without any doubt that the man was guilty and deserved imprisonment or execution.

However, just before the sentence was pronounced, the defense attorney made a statement I will not soon forget. He said something like this: "This man was a good soldier. He served faithfully in the military. He has always been a good citizen. He went to war knowing that he might one day give his life for his country. He fought valiantly and then was captured. He was brainwashed, physically tortured, and starved near to death. He suffered all the indignities of a prisoner of war year after year. Finally, after five years, six months, and four days of being tortured and brainwashed, he broke and gave his captors the information they desired. True, he did give the enemy military secrets, and he did provide confessions that were treasonous. However, had he been released after five years, six months, and three days he would have received a hero's welcome. There should be a time limit to how long a man can hold out. Year after year for five years he never wavered. Through all those days and months of suffering he maintained his loyalty to his country. Finally he broke. Can't we please give him some special consideration and leniency for his courage for five years and six months?"

This was a powerful argument and surely caused the thought processes to be stretched. Does not life involve us in a series of time limits? Imagine what would happen in athletics if there were no time limit. Basketball and football would not be the same if the teams played until they were tired or mutually agreed to stop. When time runs out in an athletic contest, whichever team is ahead is declared the winner. Vince Lombardi said, "We never lose a game—we just run out of time when the other team is ahead. We know that if we could keep playing we would eventually win." Having time limits is great motivation to achieving our greatest possible limit before the time is past.

The Lord sent a deliverer to his people. His name was Samson. The angel of the Lord told Samson's mother and father before his birth that "no razor shall come on his head: for the child shall be a Nazarite unto God from the womb: and he shall begin to deliver Israel out of the hand of the Philistines." (Judges 13:5.)

We remember reading about Samson's great strength. With his bare hands he killed a lion. He caught three hundred foxes and tied firebrands between the tails of two of them, setting the firebrands on fire. The foxes then ran into the fields of corn burning the shocks, the standing corn, the vineyards, and the olives. Another time he slew one thousand Philistines with the jawbone of an ass. Samson's strength was a God-given blessing and demanded absolute compliance with the angel's direction. Later, Delilah wanted to know the source of so great a strength. Twice he gave her false information and twice she turned him over to the Philistines, who found that he had not told the truth. Delilah "pressed him daily with her words, and urged him, so that his soul was vexed unto death." (Judges 16:16.) He finally told her all that was in his heart; he said that a razor had never come upon his head, and that if he were shaven, his strength would be gone and he would become weak like any other man. Once again Delilah turned him over to the Philistines, but because his strength was gone, they were able to put out both eyes, so that he could not see. Then they bound him with fetters of brass and imprisoned him. For twenty years Samson had judged Israel and kept the source of his strength as a sacred trust on his heart; but when he violated that trust, his strength was gone.

Even though in some measure Samson vindicated himself by pushing over the pillars that held up the house of the Philistines, and slew more at his death than he had slain in his life, his strength having returned, he violated his own time limit. The Lord had given him strength as long as he obeyed, but the moment he disobeyed, his strength was lost. The Lord revoked the marvelous blessings that Samson had been promised. Who knows what great deeds Samson might have gone on to accomplish had he been truer to his God than to the vexing words of an unfaithful wife?

David, whose heart was like unto God's own heart, was mighty in word and deed. His faith was pure and undefiled; he feared neither man nor beast. When he fought the Philistine he "ran to the battle." He was as unsullied and undefiled as the meadows and hills where he tended his father's sheep. The clear air filled his lungs and mind; the sun, wind, and rain cleansed and tempered his body. The God of heaven, even Jehovah, blessed him and loved him. Chosen by the Lord and called by Samuel the prophet, the young lad walked in the ways of the Master and committed his life to rule and bless his people.

What a blessing it would have been to David had he never seen Bathsheba. He who had soared with the eagles descended to the depths of adultery and sent Uriah "in the forefront of the hottest battle" and then had the men retire from him so that he might be smitten and die. (2 Samuel 11:15.)

David was one of God's very elect. Had there been a time limit in his life, and had it ended before this deed, undoubtedly David would have been exalted, for he had lived a lifetime of righteousness, love, and devotion. But a good man—yea, a great man—had fallen because of lust. If only his integrity could have carried him over this gulf of sin.

In our own lives we often wonder how long we can hold out. Is there a time limit? We have been taught that we must endure to the end. A lifetime of good deeds can often be eradicated by one act. Trust and confidence are lost. Reputations and character are spoiled. Opportunities to lead and serve are missed. Callings to walk in high places are forever lost.

The prophet Amulek said, "Do not procrastinate the day of your repentance until the end; for after this day of life, which is given us to prepare for eternity, behold, if we do not improve our time while in this life, then cometh the night of darkness wherein there can be no labor performed." (Alma 34:33.)

Now is the time to repent, before it is everlastingly too late. Now is the time to choose to have the faith to endure to the end. In the last verse of the third chapter of Ecclesiastes we read: "Wherefore I perceive that there is nothing better, than that a man should rejoice in his own works; for that is his portion: for who shall bring him to see what shall be after him?" (Ecclesiastes 3:22.)

How many times do you think Samson and David have re-lived the harm of their fall? How many times will it be re-

67

hearsed over and over again in eternity with the realization that everything in eternity hung in the balance and they made the wrong choice in a moment of weakness?

There is a time limit, and it is until the last breath of this life. If we do well, we will have kept our second estate.

Chapter Eleven

Preparing Ourselves
Through Prayer

Have you ever stood at the foot of a great mountain, weary and exhausted, but knowing full well that the mountain must be scaled? Vince Lombardi said, "Fatigue makes cowards of us all." If we were fresh, the obstacle would not look so great.

Many years ago when I was a young man, a group of friends and I decided to climb the north side of Mount Olympus, a tall peak overlooking the Salt Lake Valley. The temperature that day was one hundred degrees. To reach the mountain, we had to climb a rather large rock formation and then cross a deep chasm. We started out from the boulevard below the mountain and worked our way through the scrub oak and brush, then climbed to the top of the rock formation only to find we had to climb precariously down into the chasm before we could proceed up the mountain. After this obstacle some of the group decided not to continue on. The rest of us went ahead and, several hours later, in the heat of the noonday sun, finally arrived at the top. Our water was gone, the dry heat had dehydrated us greatly, and we were exhausted. After resting a bit, we ran and stumbled down the west side of the mountain, which was a fairly easy trail to follow. When we came to water at the bottom of the mountain, we drank deeply, for we had a great deal to replace.

A few years later, a friend was lost on the same mountain. The ward planned a search party. We arrived at Mount Olympus at five o'clock in the morning and began to search the north side. After several hours of intense searching, we suddenly realized that we were standing on top of Mount Olympus. What a contrast from the previous experience! We were tired, but not exhausted. We were thirsty, but not totally dehydrated. We had energy left to continue the search for several more hours. What made the difference? The objective, the cause, the reason. These were vastly different. In the latter experience, a human life was in jeopardy. Our objective of finding our friend kept us driving onward without thought of self.

Each of us also has mental and emotional mountains to climb. It is normal to have difficulties in life. The well-adjusted person meets them head on and simply starts mentally working toward the objective.

Now, let me apply the principle of prayer as a parallel. When I pray it is usually repetitive. Every time I kneel down I pray for my wife, children, and grandchildren by name. I always pray for our beloved prophet and the other Brethren. I pray faithfully for all of our missionaries, for their personal welfare, and for their protection from the evil one. I pray for our great country, and I pray that doors to other nations will be opened.

Of the last thousand prayers that I have offered, the above items would have been prayed for a thousand times. Repetition? Of course, but sincere repetition. The Lord is offended by vain repetition. Vain repetition, I think, is when we kneel down and say, "Our Heavenly Father," and then we say words that are repetitious and habitual, but our minds are on what we are going to do after we pray, or what we are going to do the next day, or what is going on in the other room while we are praying. Heavenly Father finds out that we really didn't want to talk to him.

Have you ever wondered what it would be like to have an interview with one of the General Authorities? First, you would need an appointment to discuss your problem with your bishop; he would then take the problem to the stake president, and only if they could not solve it would they take it to the Regional Representative. Then he would discuss it with the General Authority executive administrator. In other words, it would be extremely difficult, and not the order of the Church, to bypass all local priesthood leaders and go directly to a General Authority. On the other hand, have you ever really comprehended what it means to kneel in the presence of the Almighty God, the Great Elohim, the Supreme Ruler in heaven and earth? And how wonderful that we can kneel in his presence anytime night or day, twenty-four hours a day. His interest is always the same. His love is not selective or arbitrary, nor is it measured. Rather, it is absolute to each one of us. He may be displeased with what we are doing, but his love always surrounds us.

There are times when we need to sufficiently humble ourselves before the Lord. Mahonri Moriancumer, King Benjamin, Nephi, Abraham, and Moroni all practiced this principle. In fact, all of the prophets of all ages have practiced it.

Consider an introduction to prayer such as this: "Our Father who art in heaven, I kneel before thee this day in deepest solemn gratitude. I realize I am as nothing, less than the dust of the earth, the least of all thy servants, the weakest of the weak. I humble myself before thee as dust and ashes, unworthy even to approach thee."

I believe it pleases the Lord for us to come before him with this type of humility. It isn't false humility; we are not praying thus to impress others, for we are all alone with him. Therefore, we are not expecting others to say, "My, you are humble." We don't want that. We want him to know. We know and he knows, as Huckleberry Finn says, "You can't pray a lie." I think the Lord appreciates our humbling ourselves sufficiently before him. Then we express our gratitude, and then we implore him.

In our lives each of us must face a mountain to climb. It may

71

be a financial crisis, a great soul-shaking illness of a loved one, or some other great test. During those trying times a prayer might be worded like this: "Heavenly Father, I have come to a mountain I can't climb. I have thought about it, I have studied it, I have read the scriptures. I have counseled with many about it, and I simply cannot solve this problem. The mountain is too big. I can't get over it; I can't climb this one. Please, I am asking for help. No, I am not asking—I am pleading, I'm begging. Please, please, dear God, help me."

In that moment, I promise you that it would be as though he would say, "Take my hand in yours; I will walk with you all the way. I am not going to take away the problem, because I want you to grow. Trust in me and I will take you down streets you never would have dreamed. I will take you through doors you would have thought impossible, and I will cause you to speak beautifully, eloquent words of truth. You will serve in places you never would have supposed. I will walk with you all the way to the mountain's top. I will never forsake you. Have faith and trust."

President Harold B. Lee said, "The greatest test in this life is the loss of a loved one." I would add that the greatest burden is sin. The greatest bondage is debt. Each of us has faced or will face difficult situations. When those times of soul-shaking experiences come, each of us can turn to deep, meaningful, sincere prayer.

I testify that the great being we affectionately call our Father in heaven, that being who is the supreme and all-powerful Almighty God, the Great Elohim, will, with love and tenderness and absolute compassion, give us answer to our prayers.

Chapter Twelve

When Trials Come

Sometimes people excuse their own thoughtlessness toward others by rationalizing and pointing out how much greater are their own trials and problems. True charity, or love of Christ, requires that we love our neighbor at all times, regardless of how convenient or inconvenient it may be. Those who bear their own trials and afflictions gracefully and who lose themselves in service to others have been promised great blessings. The prophet Alma made this great statement in his counsel to his son Helaman: " . . . for I do know that whosoever shall put their trust in God shall be supported in their trials, and their troubles, and their afflictions, and shall be lifted up at the last day."

When faced with great difficulty, the man of faith turns to God in anxious prayer, pleading, begging, and asking for help. There are those who have been down the long road of trials who have found the rocks and crevices where peace may be lodged and where a heavy heart may be unburdened. Each one of us—every man, woman, and child—will be measured by our ability to go through these trials and still prove faithful and worthy.

I have a young friend who has been sorely tried in this life. Grasping for life itself, he made a tremendous study and finally came to a sweet peace within himself concerning his trials. His research took him through the scriptures and the writings of some of the great apostles and prophets, and he gleaned from these men of strength and integrity, men who have suffered and have been tried, the strength to endure. We all, like this young man, suffer sooner or later seeming tragedies in our lives. Our ability to brace ourselves against the winds of trial, against the storms of depression, frustration, and heartache, will eventually determine our contribution to society and mankind.

Lorenzo Snow said, "The trials and temptations have been very great to many of our people, and more or less, perhaps to all of us. The Lord seems to require some proof on our part of something to show that he can depend on us when he wants us to accomplish certain things in his interest. It is interesting that in each stake and ward the bishop comes to know soon those whom he can depend upon, those who have been through the refiner's fire, those who have been purged and cleansed, and who are as steady as God's laws upon the earth."

President Snow also said: "We are here that we may be educated in a school of suffering and of fiery trials, which school was necessary for Jesus, our elder brother, who the scriptures tell us was made perfect through suffering. It is necessary that we suffer in all things that we may be qualified and worthy to rule and govern all things, even as our Father in Heaven and his eldest son, Jesus."

If we had the privilege, we might determine that we would eliminate pain from our lives. We might determine that trials be placed elsewhere but not upon us. In our prayers we often ask that we be delivered from temptation, that our families be protected and safeguarded, that health abide in each one, that no accident may befall any of our loved ones; we pray also for the welfare of those who are sick within our family circles, and we plead that our trials may be lifted.

It has been my experience through the years to have had the privilege of speaking at many funerals, to be invited to administer to gravely ill persons, and to counsel with those who have been heavyhearted, frustrated, and perplexed. Over the years as I have seen life after life refined by these experiences, I have felt a renewed love for the testing through which we go.

Several years ago I read the biography of Wilford Woodruff. What an impact that story had on my life! President Woodruff said:

December 3rd found my wife very low. I spent the day in taking care of her, and the day following I returned to Eaton to get some things for her. She seemed to be sinking gradually, and in the evening the spirit apparently left her body, and she was dead. The sisters gathered around, weeping, while I stood looking at her in sorrow. The spirit and power of God began to rest upon me until, for the first time during her sickness, faith filled my soul, although she lay before me as one dead.

I had some oil that was consecrated for my anointing while in Kirtland. I took it and consecrated it again before the Lord, for anointing the sick. I then bowed down before the Lord, prayed for the life of my companion, and in the name of the Lord anointed her body with oil. I then laid my hands upon her, and in the name of Jesus Christ I rebuked the power of death and of the destroyer, and commanded the same to depart from her and the spirit of life to enter her body. Her spirit returned to her body, and from that hour she was made whole; and we all felt to praise the name of God, and to trust in Him and keep His commandments.

While I was undergoing this ordeal (as my wife related afterwards) her spirit left her body, and she saw it lying upon the bed and the sisters there weeping. She looked at them and at me, and upon her babe; while gazing upon this scene, two persons came into the room, carrying a coffin, and told her they had come for her body. One of these messengers said to her that she might have her choice—she might go to rest in the spirit world, or, upon one condition, she could have the privilege of returning to her tabernacle and continuing her labors upon the earth. The condition was that if she felt she could stand by her husband, and with him pass through all the cares, trials, tribulations, and afflictions of life which he would be called upon to pass through for the gospel's sake unto the end, she might return. When she looked at the situation of her husband and child, she said, "Yes, I will do it." At the moment that decision

75

was made, the power of faith rested upon me, and when I administered to her, her spirit reentered her tabernacle. (Matthias F. Cowley, *Wilford Woodruff*, Bookcraft, 1964, pp. 97-98.)

What were some of the trials through which Sister Woodruff would go? When her little daughter died, she was bowed down with grief. President Woodruff records the following letter from her, bearing the sorrowful tidings:

My Dear Wilford: What will be your feelings when I say that yesterday I was to witness the departure of our little Sarah Emma from this world? Yes, she is gone. The relentless hand of death has snatched her from my embrace. She was too lovely, kind, and affectionate to live in this wicked world. When looking upon her I have often thought how I should feel to part with her. I thought I could not live without her, especially in the absence of my companion; but she is gone. The Lord has taken her home to Himself, for some wise purpose. It is a trial to me, but the Lord has stood by me in a wonderful manner. He will take better care of her than I possibly could do. We have one little angel in heaven, and I think it likely that her spirit has visited you before this time. She used to call her Papa, and left a kiss for her Papa before she died. Today, little Wilford and I with a number of friends, came over to Commerce, to pay our last respects to our darling in seeing her decently buried. She had no relatives to follow her to the grave, or shed for her a silent tear, except her Mama and little Wilford. She lies alone in peace. "The Lord giveth, and the Lord taketh away. Blessed be the name of the Lord." Phoebe W. Woodruff. (Ibid., p. 152.)

I wonder if Sister Woodruff even had the slightest inkling of the kinds of tests with which she would be tried as companion to the beloved prophet?

President Harold B. Lee said, "The all-important thing is not that tragedies and sorrows come into our lives, but what we do with them. Death of a loved one is the most severe test that you will ever face, and if you can rise above your griefs and if you will trust in God, then you will be able to surmount any other difficulty with which you may be faced." (*Ye Are the Light of the World*, Deseret Book, 1974, p. 257.) There are many ways one can lose a loved one. Sometimes death is the sweetest. Those who have been through divorce and have seen their children, husband, or wife leave that which is most precious and dear, turn their backs away from the tree of life, and reach down into murky, filthy waters and partake of that which is forbidden understand why death is sweeter. There is a peace that comes to those who are left behind to mourn when the one taken by death has lived a righteous and a noble life, the peace that surpasseth that understanding which the Savior promised would come.

To those who sorrow Elder Mark E. Petersen has said, "Death is a beautiful doorway into a more beautiful life." President Hugh B. Brown said, "Death is not the end. It is the putting out the candle because the dawn has come." President N. Eldon Tanner, in a beautiful funeral service discourse, said, "Death is going from one place to another. There is no exit that is not also an entrance." President Lee said, "Death is so untimely. Whom would we trust to choose the hour of demise? When will we be willing to part with a loved one? Who would we have measure our life?" Kahlil Gibran said, "The cavity created by the suffering through which we go becomes a receptacle for compensating blessings." And we read in Ecclesiastes the following great message:

To every thing there is a season, and a time to every purpose under the heaven:
A time to be born, and a time to die; a time to plant, and a time to pluck up that which is planted;
A time to kill, and a time to heal; a time to break down, and a time to build up;
A time to weep, and a time to laugh; a time to mourn, and a time to dance;
A time to cast away stones, and a time to gather stones together; a time to embrace, and a time to refrain from embracing;
A time to get, and a time to lose; a time to keep, and a time to cast away;
A time to rend, and a time to sew; a time to keep silence, and a time to speak;
A time to love, and a time to hate; a time of war, and a time of peace. (Ecclesiastes 3:1-8.)

Life is a time, and each of us must go through many experiences before our lives end; therefore, we should try to find the time to do those things which are of most worth to us. We ought to examine our tasks and then make certain that we have all of these things lined up in their proper perspective, in their proper order of priority. We want to have eternal life as a family unit. We want to be able to extend the joys and happiness, the fullness of life into eternity, and only as we make those decisions which bring us close to the Savior can we hope to enjoy a fullness in the life to come.

Many lessons are learned by those who have been through trials. Some lose the luster of life, and they wither inside and wallow in self-pity. From the time of their testing, through the loss of a loved one or other personal problems, they simply exist. Others who have been through the same or similar experiences may hurt terribly inside, deep pangs of pain almost to the point where it is too great to bear, and yet through the love of friends who care, through the love of wise and wonderful bishops, stake presidents, and priesthood leaders, but more important, through their own self-determination, they make the necessary adjustments. The Lord blesses such persons, giving them a peace of mind and reassurance that is reflected in their countenances, and a strength that is found only in those who have endured, suffered in silence, and come out victorious.

The gospel of Jesus Christ gives us an anchor for our faith. The Savior said: "Come unto me, all ye that labour and are heavy laden, and I will give you rest. Take my yoke upon you, and learn of me; for I am meek and lowly in heart: and ye shall find rest unto your souls. For my yoke is easy, and my burden is light." (Matthew 11:28-30.)

As we contemplate life's trials, we find that every soul on the face of the earth is tested to a greater or lesser degree. Each one of us, as someone has said, carries a cross on his or her heart. Walk down the street any day and you can meet those who carry their crosses with a light heart, who have made the necessary adjustments and have determined to accept the cross and carry it as best they can. For others you see, the burden is oppressive. They can hardly walk; their facial features are strained; they do not have energy left to fight the battle of life; they have no enthusiasm for life's great blessings.

Dr. Albert Schweitzer said, "Don't vex your mind by trying to explain the suffering you have to endure in this life. Don't think God is punishing or disciplining you or that he has rejected you. Even in the midst of your suffering, you are in his kingdom. You are always his child and he has his protecting arms around you. Does a child understand everything his father does? No, but he can confidently nestle in his father's arms and feel perfect happiness even while tears glisten in his eyes because he is his father's child."

We have a sweet, loving Heavenly Father who, as we come to him, will cradle us in his arms in his mercy and in his love. Knowing that he loves us, that he wants that which is best for us, should give us peace enough. Someone has said, "The sun with all the planets rotating around it can ripen the smallest bunch of grapes as though it had nothing else to do." With our limited understanding it may seem impossible for us that God could behold every particle of the earth, yea, millions of earths like this, that he could in an instant comprehend the thoughts of us all. Enoch, who had the Spirit of the Lord fall upon him, beheld this world, and there was not a particle of it that he did not behold, "and his heart swelled wide as eternity." (Moses 7:41.) God's heart is as wide as eternity. He will wrap us in his love even as a mother wraps her young infant child in her arms.

In 1921 Margaret Widdemer wrote about one mother function under the title of *The Watcher.* She said:

> *She always leaned to watch for us,*
> *Anxious if we were late,*
> *In winter by the window,*
> *In summer by the gate;*
> *And though we mocked her tenderly,*
> *Who had such foolish care,*

The long way home would seem more safe
Because she waited there.

Her thoughts were all so full of us,
She never could forget!
And so I think that where she is
She must be watching yet.
Waiting till we come home to her
Anxious if we are late—
Watching from heaven's window
Leaning from heaven's gate.

Likewise, we have a God who leans and watches from heaven's gate who will never let us be tempted above that which we are able, who will never let us suffer beyond that which we can endure, who will let us place our hand in his and walk with him through this life, knowing full well that trials and tests will come and that he will have to depart from us for a time until we go through the test and come out the other side.

I have always been opposed to those who take tranquilizers during the heavy trials of their lives. We don't want to tranquilize out of our lives the deep hurts or suffering. Those who tranquilize during the period of the funeral and through the periods of trial eventually must have the suffering, and generally it is not when loved ones are near as they are at a funeral; oftentimes it comes weeks and months after. Generally it is easier to suffer during the time we have our loved ones around us than to put it off or procrastinate it until another time.

President Tanner has said, "The only acceptable length of life is eternal life." And in the Doctrine and Covenants, we read the following:

"Hearken, O ye people of my church, to whom the kingdom has been given; hearken ye and give ear to him who laid the foundation of the earth, who made the heavens and all the hosts thereof, and by whom all things were made which live, and move, and have a being.

"And again I say, hearken unto my voice, *lest death shall*

80

overtake you; in an hour when ye think not the summer shall be past, and the harvest ended, and your souls not saved." (D&C 45:1-2. Italics added.)

Let us in this life face adversity, face trial, face the perplexities and frustrations of life with an eye on that distant goal of eternal life. There is a God in heaven. He is our spiritual father. He has a supreme interest in us, for he has said, "This is my work and my glory—to bring to pass the immortality and eternal life of man." (Moses 1:39.) Our advocate with God the Eternal Father is Jesus Christ, the Redeemer, the Atoner, the great I Am, the God of Israel. And as we trust in him, we find that our burdens are made light, that we find peace for the soul.

Let us choose to live a life of service—to live outside ourselves, to fulfill the measure of our creation. And for those who will suffer, who may be tempted, who may be tested, who may be bowed down and heavyhearted, who oftentimes suffer in silence, remember that no matter how dark the night, the dawn is irresistible. Truly, light will come and there will be glorious days ahead. God bless you. I pray with all my heart and soul that in your time of trial, the Lord will encircle you about with his angels, priesthood holders will be there to give special blessings when needed, your prayers will ascend to a kind and loving Father, and you will find the peace and comfort and courage to endure. God bless us all to do so, that we might have the only acceptable life, eternal life, with our loved ones.

Chapter Thirteen

Acres of Diamonds

Many times during his ministry on earth, Jesus taught, "Thou shalt love thy neighbour as thyself." (Matthew 19:19.) Before we can practice true charity toward our neighbor, each of us must find himself, learn to accept himself for what he is and, more importantly, for what he can become.

To illustrate this point, may I share with you a memorable story by Russell Conwell, titled *Acres of Diamonds.* In it, the author tells of being in Baghdad and hiring an old Arab guide. With a camel train they went down the Tigris and Euphrates rivers. As they walked along the banks of these rivers, they saw beautiful white sands, and the old Arab guide told story after story, somewhat like a modern-day barber. "Finally, instead of acting as if I weren't listening," Conwell said, "I'd act as if I were listening and then just turn him off. I guess he noticed this, because all of a sudden he took his turban off and waved it around to get my attention, but I just ignored him. He kept waving, and pretty soon I succumbed to the temptation and looked over at him. As soon as I did, he started into a story. He said, 'This story I save for my particular friends.' Then he told me this story:

In ancient Persia there was a man by the name of Ali Hafid who owned orchards, gardens, and fields of grain. Ali Hafid was rich. He was contented because he was wealthy, and he was wealthy because he was contented. One day a Buddhist priest came by Ali Hafid's home, and together they sat by the fire. This Buddhist priest told how the Almighty put his finger in a bank of fog and started whirling it around faster and faster until it burst into a solid mass of flame. And then it went rolling off through the universe. As it did, it went through other fog banks, and the dew settled on the earth, and the crust began to form. As it formed, after it had gone through fog bank after fog bank, some of the inner eruption came forth. The priest said, "This is where we got our mountains and hills and our valleys and our deep gorges. This is the thing that beautified the earth. As the earth's crust cooled, that which cooled most rapidly was granite; less rapidly, copper; then silver, gold, and last of all diamonds." And the priest said to Ali Hafid, "If you had a diamond as big as your thumb, you could buy this whole country. If you had a diamond mine, you could place your children on thrones throughout the world."

After the Buddhist priest had left, Ali Hafid went to bed. He was a poor man. He was poor because he was discontented, and he was discontented because he felt and feared that he was poor. He didn't sleep all that night, and when the morning came, he arose early and went over to the Buddhist priest's home and said to him, "I must find a diamond mine. Where should I look for one?"

The Buddhist priest, having been awakened early in the morning and not feeling too pleasant, said, "You look for a river between high mountains, and the river will flow on white sands, and there you will find diamonds."

"There isn't any such place."

"There is," replied the priest, "and there are many of them, and you will find them. You will always find diamonds."

Ali Hafid answered, "Then I will go." And he went home and sold his farm and collected the money. Then he left his family with a nearby neighbor and went on his search for diamonds. He started in the Mountains of the Moon, and then he went down into Palestine, and finally over into Europe. Many years later—in wretched poverty, having been driven all the way across Europe, not a penny left, in rags, heartsick, weary, tired—he stood on the bay of Barcelona. As a giant tide came in between the Pillars of Hercules, unable to resist the terrible temptation, he threw himself into the incoming tide and sank beneath the crest—never to rise again in this life.

The old Arab stopped telling the story and went back to

83

straighten the pack on the camel's back. Then he came forward again and went right on with the next chapter.

The man who bought the farm from Ali Hafid went out to water his camel one day in the little stream that ran through the white sands of the farm. As he did, he saw something glistening in the sand. He reached down into the water and pulled a huge stone out. As he pulled it out, he noticed that it caught all the different hues of the rainbow, so he took it in the house and set it on his mantel. Three or four weeks later, the old Buddhist priest came by, entered the house, and soon spotted this rock on the mantel. He walked over and said, "Well, that's a diamond! Has Ali Hafid returned?"

"No, Ali Hafid has not returned, and that's not a diamond. It's just a rock that I found out in my stream here."

"That is a diamond! I know diamonds!" the priest replied. So they went out and dug in the sands nearby, and with almost every shovelful of sand, they turned up more diamonds.

The Arab concluded this story by saying that Ali Hafid's farm was the Golconda mine, the richest diamond mine in all the history of the world. If Ali Hafid had stayed home and dug in his own fields, he would have had acres of diamonds.

That's a great story relating to what I would now like to discuss: the acres of diamonds each of us has as an individual.

I had lunch recently with a man I admire very much. I have come to love him just because of his story. I had heard about him and admired him for a long time. His name is Douglas Snarr. Have you ever heard of Snarr Advertising Agency? Possibly you have seen many of his billboards; that is Douglas Snarr's business.

As a young man, Douglas Snarr developed a serious problem with stuttering and stammering. He said that when he got into high school, the stuttering became more intense, until finally he withdrew into a shell and would hardly speak in any of his classes. He remembered in particular one summer night when he went to his girlfriend's house. He went to the door and knocked. Her father came to the door and said, "What do you want, young man?"

Douglas explained how he felt at the time: "I tried to say what I wanted, but I couldn't. The words wouldn't come. The perspiration started pouring off my face, and I wanted to say something, but I still couldn't, so I just stood there. All of a sudden Carol came down the spiral staircase in a beautiful dress and said, 'Well, Daddy, that's Douglas Snarr. He's come to take me out tonight.' And with those words she took all the pressure off and alleviated the problem."

Despite his problem, Douglas decided that he had a great talent and so he developed a business. After his senior year of high school, he had earned enough money in that business to enter Brigham Young University. He came to one class, a very large class, and sat in the middle of the back row, where surely no one would call him to answer questions or do anything. The professor went down the roll and said, "We'd like to have Douglas Snarr come up and give the opening prayer."

Doug said, "I made my way to the aisle and walked down to the front of the class and stood there with my head bowed. I wanted to pray, but the words wouldn't come. I'd have given anything, but they still wouldn't come. Then the pressure became more intense. Perspiration ran down my face. I could feel it under my arms. The pressure was absolutely intense. Finally the professor got up, came over and stood by me, put his arm around me, and said, 'I will give the prayer.' And he gave the prayer. As I made my way back to my seat, no one wanted to look at me because they didn't want to embarrass me. But it was irresistible; they had to look. I felt like a freak. After class this kind professor came to me and said, 'Doug, if you will continue to come to class, I'll make it worth your while. We think we've got something that will be worthwhile in this class, and I promise you that I'll never call on you again.' The teacher's comment was worse because it made me feel like a spectacle."

Doug wanted to do something about his stuttering, but that just accentuated the problem. He decided he would try to find a speech correction school. He finally found one, and after he had taken a battery of tests, the speech therapist told him, "You have a severe case of stammering and stuttering." I guess the teacher didn't have to be a genius to tell him that. The man who conducted the tests said to him, "We really don't know all that much about stammering and stuttering for a case as severe as yours. We don't know what we can really do for you, Doug, but I will tell you this: we can teach you how to live with the problem."

Doug described his reaction:

Something welled up inside me that made me so mad I could hardly stand it. I didn't want to *live* with the problem. I turned to the man and said, "You're no good!" Then I turned and left. I was heartsick.

I went through school that year, and then one day when I was sitting in a barber chair, I saw a little ad in the paper about a man in Chicago who would guarantee speech correction in a course costing one thousand dollars. I told my dad I would like to go to this speech school in Chicago, and he had BYU and Utah State University and the University of Utah check it out. They all told him that the teacher was a quack, that he really couldn't do anything, and that the course was just a waste of money. So I decided I would pay for the course myself. I went back home that summer and, although there was a girl I was interested in, I didn't go on one date. I worked that whole summer and finally earned enough.

When I went to Chicago, I found the school, went in, and was met by a seventy-four-year-old man. He said, "When I was your age I had a problem very similar to yours. You can overcome the problem and someday you'll speak as I am speaking." I started to cry because somebody had told me I didn't have to live with my problem.

For the first ten days of the course, we could not say one word. (I should mention that we met in a shabby little room—gray, dull, dingy—and one of the women who taught was about the same age as the man and was blind.) At the end of ten days, they taught me to move my arm back and forth slowly while saying, "My name is Doug Snarr." I want to tell you what that was to be able to speak! I didn't mind moving my arm because I was finally communicating. I was saying something, and it was coming out! We started speaking slowly, then picked up the pace. I used to go out and sit in the park with a newspaper. There would be drunks and others lying on benches, but I'd put the newspaper over my arm and read or talk to myself, with my arm moving back and forth under the paper with every syllable—practicing.

Then, one Sunday about nine weeks later, I had a regression. I didn't know what to do, so I knelt down. I have prayed most of my life, but this day I really prayed: "Dear God, help me to know what to do." Then the message came, so I got up from my knees, called a taxi, and went down to the LDS chapel. It was too late; church was out, and the building was locked up. In a little note on the front door, the branch president had left his name and address. I went back to the taxi and told the driver to take me to that address. When I arrived I rang the doorbell, and a man came to the door with his little girl right behind him. I stammered, "My-name-is-Doug-Snarr. I've-prayed-and-God-has-sent-me-to-you."

The little girl went running to her mother and said, "Mother, come quick. There's a crazy man at the door talking to daddy." (I was eighteen at the time.) You can imagine how I felt. Anyway, the branch president invited me in, we talked for a while, and he said, "Go out and send the taxi away. We will take you home tonight. Tomorrow you pack your things and come and live with us the whole time you are in Chicago."

A short time later, this family took me on a trip to southern Illinois. I talked to one of the members of the Church there, waving my arm but carrying on a regular conversation. The woman said, "You know, Doug, you've got a great story to tell. I think you ought to tell it at church." Although I said I didn't think I could do it, she continued, "Do it, Doug. You come and speak to our people. They need to hear it."

Charity is the pure love of Christ, when you don't mind being embarrassed, when all you can think about is the good of of the people. And so Doug said "All right, I'll speak at your sacrament meeting." The night before his talk, Doug hardly slept at all. Then at the meeting he was just as nervous as he could possibly be until the bishop finally called on him to speak. He stood up, put his arm out, and then put it down. He gave the whole talk without moving his arm. His problem was solved. If you could hear Douglas Snarr talk today, you would find that he speaks about as fast as I do, and I speak very fast. He has an exciting way of speaking, without the slightest trace of a problem.

Let me tell you just one other thing about Douglas Snarr, because I know that his ability to speak is a miracle. He is very successful, and he's been a pusher—a driver. He just cannot believe that anyone can't succeed if he wants to succeed. All he has to do is make his own rules and then live by them, and he will succeed. Doug was in Washington, D.C., some time ago, riding in a taxicab. The driver, who was black, pulled up beside a bus. The bus driver looked down, saw this black driver, and started trying to force him off the road. Doug asked, "What's going on here?" The driver answered, "I guess this guy doesn't like blacks."

The taxi driver slowed down, and the bus went on down the street. When the taxi tried to pass the bus again, the bus driver swerved right over in front of it. Doug said, "I can't believe this." Finally, both vehicles pulled up to a red light. Doug jumped out of the back seat of the taxi and ran around to the window of the bus. He reached in, grabbed the bus driver, and started pulling him down. The driver slammed the window shut on Doug's arm, and when Doug pulled it out it was bleeding down his white shirt and his suit. He then ran around to the door and saw that it was locked. Then he stood about six inches in front of the bus. When the light turned green, the driver started inching up until the bus window was right against Doug's nose. Doug wouldn't move, so the bus driver stopped. Horns were honking, and pretty soon a policeman came over and asked, "What's going on here?"

Doug answered, "This man tried to force that black driver off the road. He tried to cause an accident. He didn't care; he's just prejudiced. I want to talk to him."

Finally the bus driver opened the door, and the policeman got on to talk to him and the people on the bus. The passengers agreed that the driver had been trying to force the black cabbie off the road. Then the policeman said to the driver, "We will report this to your company and take appropriate action."

The bus driver started to cry. He said, "I have a family. This is all I've done all my life. If I'm fired from this, I don't know what I'll do."

And then Doug said, "If you'll go over and apologize to that black driver, it will all be forgotten." So the bus driver went over and apologized to the black driver and got back in his bus, and it was all forgotten. Then Doug climbed into the back of the taxi, and the black driver turned around—tears in his eyes—and said, "That's the first time in my life that anyone has ever stuck up for me."

What I am trying to do is help you to realize that we each have our own acres of diamonds, no matter what the problem is. I told some seminary students the other day about an experience I had after getting glasses. I hadn't worn them all my life, so they changed my appearance a little bit. I was in a store, and one of our neighbors came in, a woman about my age. She looked at me and said, "Is that you? Is that really you? Vaughn Featherstone, is that you?"

I said, "Yes, why?"

"Well, I thought you had on horn-rimmed glasses and a plastic nose!"

I said, "No, that's my nose." And then I said, "I have one advantage over you: I take one breath and it lasts me all day."

After hearing this story, quite a few of the seminary students came up to shake hands. Then one girl came up, stood back and looked at me, and said, "You know, you don't really have a big nose." I answered, "You're a sweetheart."

There are those kinds of people who help others feel as if their idiosyncrasies really aren't all that much of a problem. I can't do anything about my nose, and I think if we were to look around we'd find people who think their legs are bigger than they ought to be, or smaller than they ought to be. Maybe their shoulders are slumped instead of squared. Maybe their noses are bigger than they'd like, or maybe their ears are too big. Many things can't be changed, and we have to live with them. It doesn't matter what the problems are; we can overcome any of them if we just understand that we are creations of God, and each of us is somebody. We're going someplace, and we can make real contributions to the kingdom as soon as we start looking outside ourselves instead of thinking only about ourselves and all the problems we have.

I have a formula for success that I quote quite often :

When you want a thing bad enough to go out and fight for
   it,
To work day and night for it,
To give up your peace and your sleep and your time for it;
If only the desire of it makes your aim strong enough never
   to tire of it;
If life seems all empty and useless without it,
And all that you dream and you scheme is about it;
If gladly you'll sweat for it, fret for it, plan for it,
Pray with all your strength for it;
If you'll simply go after the thing that you want with all
   your capacity,
Strength and sagacity; faith, hope, and confidence, stern
   pertinacity;
If neither poverty nor cold nor famish nor gaunt
Nor sickness of pain to body or brain can turn you away
   from the aim
That you want;
If dogged and grim, you besiege and beset it, you'll get it!

Isn't that easy? That's all you have to do if you want to be a success!

I have collected several quotations of successful men concerning what they think the secrets of achievement are. Thomas Edison said, "Geniuses themselves don't talk about the gift of genius. They talk about hard work and long hours." He also said, "Genius is one percent inspiration and ninety-nine percent perspiration." Michelangelo said, "If people knew how hard I work to get my mastery, it wouldn't seem so wonderful at all." And Paderewski said, "A genius? Perhaps, but before I was a genius I was a drudge." Alexander Hamilton said, "All the genius I may have is merely the fruit of labor and thought." Dorothea Brande wrote a whole book, *Wake Up and Live*, to get across one simple formula for success: "Act as though it were impossible to fail." Shouldn't we in God's kingdom act as though it were impossible to fail? There is no reason to fail.

90

I picked up another interesting quotation from a fellow who was also a stutterer. His idea kind of wraps up what Doug said about his experience: "You see, I'm a stutterer, and I've spent twenty-five years of my life doing a pretty good job of it. During that time I learned a great many tricks to avoid speaking. I even avoided trying to speak or taking a chance. I was afraid of failure, which could compound itself eventually into total retreat from reality. Failure can be overcome, but a fear of failure can suck the lifeblood from a person's ego and leave him useless to himself, his family, and his company."

If a person will be a trainer of people, or a teacher, or a philosopher, he needs to plant the sweet smell of success in the nostrils of those he would inspire. Others must be able to see some vision out ahead. We need to remember a great phrase by President Hugh B. Brown: "No matter how dark the night, the dawn is irresistible." Isn't there something splendid about light? In the gospel, as we gain a great deal of light, we can then judge good and evil. But as we start doing the things that cause the Spirit to withdraw from us, we lose our ability to judge.

Each of us oftentimes thinks: "I have problems. I am nobody." The competition is keen in the world today. Every person must be tested. Every person must be tried. President Harold B. Lee said, "The greatest test we have in this life is the loss of a loved one, and the greatest burden we carry is sin." Any of us may have a problem like that, or a physical ailment of some kind that causes us not to be all we think we ought to be. If we only knew some of the great people of the earth and what they have accomplished, if we could look back and see the obstacles they had, we would be so grateful to have all that we have. No matter what the problems are—physically, mentally, or in any way—we'd say, "I am grateful, dear God, that I am what I am and that I have all these things." We ought to start looking for the positives in our lives instead of the negatives.

I remember the story of a famous artist who painted a beautiful portrait. He stood in front of it, looked at it for a long time, and then started to weep. A person nearby saw him and

91

asked, "What's the matter? Why are you weeping? Isn't it satisfactory? Aren't you satisfied with it?" The artist replied, "That is the problem. I am satisfied with it." What the artist had just discovered was that, if he was satisfied with the picture, he didn't know how to improve. He didn't have enough concept, skill, or ability to increase and improve that painting. I think it was Michelangelo, blind and reaching his ninetieth year, who said as he felt a sculpture that someone else had done, "Even at ninety I continue to learn." This is a great life, and it is a marvelous time to live. The Lord has said, "If ye are prepared ye shall not fear." (D&C 38:30.)

I am just so excited to live in this day and to be part of the wrapping-up process, I can't tell you what it means to me to be on the Savior's team in this very critical day. I guess, if I had my "druthers," I would hope that my family could be spared from all the filth and pornography and all the garbage on the newsstands and the things we see in the movies. They can if they're trained properly and if they have self-discipline. We are all going to be subjected to these things, but we can live the kind of life that would draw us close to the Savior and help us to be the kind of people we ought to be—once we make the decision to do it.

Chapter Fourteen

Walking in His Steps

Some time ago I heard a story about a young woman who was a voracious reader and had a study filled with books. Each night she would come home from work and read from books in her library, and she always finished every book she picked up.

One night she came to a particularly interesting crossroads. She had decided that she would read a book she had been especially avoiding, so finally she picked it up, sat down, and began to read. It was very dull and uninteresting, but she had vowed she would never read a book without finishing it; so she continued, night after night, until she finally completed it. As she replaced it on the bookshelf, she made this mental note to herself: *That was the dullest book I have ever read!*

Some time later she was out with a gentleman friend, and after dinner, he asked if she had ever read such and such a book. The mental note came back, *That was the dullest book I have ever read!* She said to her friend, "Yes, why?" He said, "I wrote it." Then they talked about the book.

That evening after he took her home, she went to her study, pulled the book off the shelf, and read through the long hours of the night. When the first streaks of sunlight shafted across the sky, she closed the back cover of the book, placed it back on the bookshelf, and made another mental note to herself: *That was the most beautiful book I have ever read!* The difference was that she knew the author.

In the forty-fifth section of the Doctrine and Covenants, the Lord says:

> Hearken, O ye people of my church, to whom the kingdom has been given; hearken ye and give ear to him who laid the foundation of the earth, who made the heavens and all the hosts thereof, and by whom all things were made which live, and move, and have a being.
>
> And again I say, hearken unto my voice, lest death shall overtake you; in an hour when ye think not the summer shall be past, and the harvest ended, and your souls not saved.
>
> Listen to him who is the advocate with the Father, who is pleading your cause before him—
>
> Saying: Father, behold the sufferings and death of him who did no sin, in whom thou wast well pleased; behold the blood of thy Son which was shed, the blood of him whom thou gavest that thyself might be glorified;
>
> Wherefore, Father, spare these my brethren that believe on my name, that they may come unto me and have everlasting life. (D&C 45:1-5.)

We can know the Author, and so much everlasting is at stake whether or not we know him.

In my own limited schooling the subject of Jesus Christ touches my greatest area of learning. I know more and have read more about him and have served more in his cause than anything else that I have done in my life. His life is the perfect pattern for each of us.

The words of the prophets help us understand better who our Master is. Alma said:

> And behold, he shall be born of Mary, at Jerusalem which is the land of our forefathers, she being a virgin, a precious and a chosen vessel, who shall be overshadowed and conceive by the power of the Holy Ghost, and bring forth a son, yea, even the Son of God.
>
> And he shall go forth, suffering pains and afflictions and temptations of every kind; and this that the word might be fulfilled which saith he will take upon him the pains and the sicknesses of his people.

And he will take upon him death, that he may loose the bands of death which bind his people; and he will take upon him their infirmities, that his bowels may be filled with mercy, according to the flesh, that he may know according to the flesh how to succor his people according to their infirmities.

Now the Spirit knoweth all things; nevertheless the Son of God suffereth according to the flesh that he might take upon him the sins of his people, that he might blot out their transgressions according to the power of his deliverance; and now behold, this is the testimony which is in me. (Alma 7:10-13.)

And the prophet Nephi said:

And now, my beloved brethren, after ye have gotten into this straight and narrow path, I would ask if all is done? Behold, I say unto you, Nay; for ye have not come thus far save it were by the word of Christ with unshaken faith in him, relying wholly upon the merits of him who is mighty to save.

Wherefore, ye must press forward with a steadfastness in Christ, having a perfect brightness of hope, and a love of God and of all men. Wherefore, if ye shall press forward, feasting upon the word of Christ, and endure to the end, behold, thus saith the Father: Ye shall have eternal life.

And now, behold, my beloved brethren, this is the way, and there is none other way nor name given under heaven whereby man can be saved in the kingdom of God. And now, behold, this is the doctrine of Christ, and the only true doctrine of the Father, and of the Son, and of the Holy Ghost, which is one God, without end. (2 Nephi 31:19-21.)

And then, finally, Nephi concluded the last verses in 2 Nephi by saying:

And now, my beloved brethren, and also Jew, and all ye ends of the earth, hearken unto these words and believe in Christ; and if ye believe not in these words believe in Christ. And if ye shall believe in Christ ye will believe in these words, for they are the words of Christ, and he hath given them unto me; and they teach all men that they should do good. . . .

And now, my beloved brethren, all those who are of the house of Israel, and all ye ends of the earth, I speak unto you as the voice of one crying from the dust, Farewell until that great day shall come.

And you that will not partake of the goodness of God, and respect the words of the Jews, and also my words, and the words which shall proceed forth out of the mouth of the Lamb of God, behold, I bid you an everlasting farewell, for these words shall condemn you at the last day.

For what I seal on earth, shall be brought against you at the judgment bar; for thus hath the Lord commanded me, and I must obey. (2 Nephi 33:10, 13-14.)

As I have studied about the life and teachings of the Savior, I have wondered about the men who have enlisted their hearts and souls in his cause. What manner of man, indeed, could enlist in the very beginning? The man Adam, after he was driven out of the Garden of Eden, built an altar and offered sacrifice. After many days an angel of the Lord appeared unto Adam and said, "Why dost thou offer sacrifices unto the Lord?" Adam, in a formula that all of us ought to understand, simply said, "I know not, save the Lord commanded me." And the angel spoke, saying, "This thing is a similitude of the sacrifice of the Only Begotten. . . . Wherefore, thou shalt do all that thou doest in the name of the Son, and thou shalt repent and call upon God in the name of the Son forevermore." (Moses 5:6-8.) Had we no further scriptures than those simple verses, we would have the pattern for living. Yet we oftentimes need much more.

We could consider Enoch, who was slow of speech and only a lad. All of the people hated him. Later in his ministry they called him a wild man, as it has been described in the scriptures. Enoch beheld the heavens weep, and he cried to the Lord: "How is it that thou canst weep, seeing thou art holy, and from all eternity to all eternity? And were it possible that man could number the particles of the earth, yea, millions of earths like this, it would not be a beginning to the number of thy creations; and thy curtains are stretched out still; and yet thou art there, and thy bosom is there; and also thou art just; thou art merciful and kind forever; . . . how is it that thou canst weep?" (Moses 7:29-31.)

Then God let Enoch behold all the myriad of souls who have walked upon the earth. Enoch beheld their wickedness, and he beheld their misery. Finally, after he had had the privilege of seeing these through his spiritual eyes, even with the discernment of God, he cried out. His heart swelled wide as eternity. He stretched forth his arms; his bowels yearned; and all eternity shook. I believe there have been a few times when we feel something akin to how Enoch felt, when our souls are so filled with love that we understand. And so we catch from Enoch the prophet a dimension we normally would not have: heart and soul enlisted in the cause of the Master.

And Moses also—after he had beheld all things that pertain to this life and every soul who had walked the earth, who was walking the earth at that time, or who would walk the earth—after the vision had departed from Moses and he was left unto himself, he said, "Now . . . I know that man is nothing, which thing I never had supposed." (Moses 1:10.)

Well, man is something, but I suppose if we could have looked through the eyes of Moses and seen all these things—millions, yea, billions of souls who had walked the earth—we might, with Moses, have cried out, "Now I perceive that man is nothing." These kinds of things help me to understand the Savior.

The same understanding comes when we read the third chapter of Daniel, where Shadrach, Meshach, and Abednego, three of the Hebrew officers who were in the councils, were thrown into the furnace. King Nebuchadnezzar had built the marvelous golden image, threescore cubits high (about ninety feet high) and nine feet across, and placed it in the plain of Dura. Then he had all his officers, governors, counselors, and others who held any position of worth come to the dedication of the image.

Then he had his herald proclaim to all those who were there: "At what time ye hear the sound of the cornet, flute, harp, sackbut, psaltery, dulcimer, and all kinds of musick, ye fall down and worship the golden image that Nebuchadnezzar the king hath set up: And whoso falleth not down and worshippeth shall be cast into the midst of a burning fiery furnace."

And so the instruments were sounded and all those who were there bowed down before the golden image. Finally, others came to King Nebuchadnezzar and said, "O king, live for ever." Then they went on to tell the king that there were three who, when the musical instruments sounded, would not bow down before the golden image and would not worship it. King Nebuchadnezzar was wroth, and he had the three young men brought before him. Then in his wrath and fury he said to them, "Shadrach, Meshach, and Abednego, . . . if ye be ready that at what time ye hear the sound of the cornet, flute, harp, sackbut, psaltery, and dulcimer, and all kinds of musick, ye fall down and worship the image which I have made; well: but if ye worship not, ye shall be cast the same hour into the midst of a burning fiery furnace." (Daniel 3:1-15.)

Can you comprehend what is taking place? Here are three fine young Hebrew lads, and this kind of pressure is being put on them—not just a little bit of pressure, or temptation, but their lives really are hanging in the balance.

And so they responded in this manner: "O Nebuchadnezzar, we are not careful to answer thee in this matter. If it be so, our God whom we serve is able to deliver us from the burning fiery furnace, and he will deliver us out of thine hand, O king. But if not, be it known unto thee, O king, that we will not serve thy gods, nor worship the golden image which thou hast set up." (Daniel 3:16-18.)

In that hour the furnaces were heated seven times hotter than they were wont to be heated, and the mightiest men were wrapped in coats and hosen so that they might not perish in the flames. But even as they cast Shadrach, Meshach, and Abednego into the burning fiery furnace, they perished in the flames—it was so hot! Then Nebuchadnezzar, astonished, said, "Did not we cast three men bound into the midst of the fire? . . . I see four men loose, walking in the midst of the fire, and they have no hurt; and the form of the fourth is like the Son of God." (Daniel 3:1-25.)

I believe that for someone to have the kind of influence over my life and your life that He had over the lives of those three young men, there must be something substantial to which we can anchor our souls.

Think of the example of the Prophet Joseph Smith and his brother Hyrum, Willard Richards, John Taylor, and others whose lives hung in the balance. Willard Richards said to the Prophet, "Joseph, if you are condemned to die, I will die in your place." Joseph said, knowing something that many did not know at that time, "But Willard, you cannot do that." Willard Richards replied, "Yes, Joseph, but I will." Such things help us to understand the kind of men enlisted not only in the service of Joseph and the prophets, but also in the greater work of the Master.

In our own day think of President Spencer W. Kimball, whose whole life—despite open heart surgery, brain surgery, heart attack, Bell's palsy, throat surgery—whose whole life is given to service. I'm impressed with President Ezra Taft Benson, who in a great area conference in Sweden a few years ago stood up and—as a prophet would—declared to the leaders and the kings and the presidents of nations that they should accept the Lord Jesus Christ and repent. That is what you would expect a prophet of God to do.

Now, along with these things, I would like to suggest that there are certain places we arrive at when we walk in his footsteps, destinations where we wouldn't suppose life would ever lead us. Let me share with you just a few of the places walking in his steps has led me.

I remember one Christmas Eve not too many years ago when I went to spend a few moments in the home of a widow in our ward. She discussed with me the things that were on her heart that lonely Christmas Eve, and I received a little jar of jelly from her as I prepared to depart. When I found out a few months later that she was in a rest home, I dropped by occasionally and visited her there. And then again, just a few short months after that, I was privileged to speak at her funeral. Now, I suppose the greater act may have been hers, because, you see, she gave me something that I would not have had otherwise.

Other experiences include the privilege of standing by men and women and children in dire poverty whose lives were committed to Him. I've seen them feed the missionaries when all the food they had in the house was on the table, and what little was left over would go to the children—and if there was none left, the children would have none. Such was an act of Christianity, one that they could not deny, to feed the Lord's servants.

I've seen his teachings reflected in other ways. We read about the widow and her placing into the treasury her mite, I suppose embarrassed as she did so for fear that it was such a little bit to be given. Well, I saw a widow come before her bishop at tithing settlement and say, "That is my full tithing—$55." Her income, then, would have been $550, to pay taxes, buy food, take care of her phone bill, lights, and heat, and make other contributions to the Church. When you subtract the $55, you're down to $495. With a sweet, humble attitude she said, "That's all there is, bishop, but it is a full tithing." And we talk about poverty, which was then at the $4500 level and is now about $7500. I'm not certain we understand. There are those who have poverty of the soul, who have poverty of the spirit; and there are those who are rich with the spirit, as is this sweet sister.

We read about the woman who had an issue of blood—twelve years of suffering every single day. She had gone to many physicians, had spent all of her money, and was none the better—in fact, was even worse. Then she found out that Jesus would be in the streets. Watching in desperation as he came by—and I'm sure pushing herself through the multitude, thinking in her heart, "If I may touch but his clothes, I shall be whole"—pushing through the crowd, she finally reached out, touched his garment, and was healed; the blood was stanched.

The Savior stopped and said, "Who touched my clothes?" The disciples said, "Thou seest the multitude thronging thee, and sayest thou, who touched me?" Turning around and looking on the body of people near him, Jesus undoubtedly noted that this woman stood out as though she were a light globe. If I read correctly between the lines, she felt guilty, I'm sure. So she came forward, knelt before him, and simply confessed. And then he said, "Daughter, thy faith hath made thee whole." (Mark 5:24-34.) I love him for that.

I love him for other things. I love him for a phone call from Idaho. A young couple had just had twins prematurely. One of them was doing fairly well, but the other, weighing just a little over a pound and a quarter, was being brought to the University of Utah Medical Center. Think of five cubes of butter, if you will, and you're talking about the size of this little soul. I received a call: "He has been administered to, but would you mind dropping by the hospital and giving him a blessing?" I found that about the only hour I had available that particular day was at five o'clock in the morning. I dropped by the medical center at that hour, went into the room, and found the oxygen canopy. I put my fingers—all that would fit—on the forehead of this little soul, gave a blessing, and had the impression from God that one day this boy—six feet tall, two hundred pounds—would be a young ambassador for the Lord.

Some time ago as I left a conference assignment and was on the way to the airport, I met a sweet family of members. They told me about a nonmember man who was having severe problems, and wondered if I would give him a blessing. We dropped by the man's home, and in the living room of the apartment were two pieces of furniture, a bean bag and a stereo set—nothing more. A little girl, age nine, was taking care of her father because the mother, when she heard her husband had cancer, had abandoned him and their two children, the nine-year-old girl and a boy about seven years old. The girl said, "I don't think my father is expecting you. I don't think he is expecting anyone." I said, "Would you please go ask him." So she went into the bedroom, and in a minute she came out and said, "Yes, he is expecting you. Will you please come in." She

101

took us down the hallway into the bedroom, and there on a bunk we saw a man who was six feet tall and weighed only sixty-seven pounds. We administered to him, feeling he would not live. But we felt impressed to bless him with the thing that would be of most worth to him: that his son and daughter would be protected, that angels would walk through this life with them, that they would be watched over when he wasn't there to do it any longer. Such kinds of experiences can't be bought for all the money in the world.

Some time ago I had the privilege of being involved with a young man and his father. The youth and a friend had been hiking in the foothills near Cody, Wyoming. The friend jumped across a high-power line that was down, but the young man got tangled in it and was electrocuted. The friend ran all the way back down to where the father lived—and it wasn't a short distance—and told the father that his son had been electrocuted and was dead. The father, who was not a young man, ran all the way back up, taking about fifteen minutes. When he got to where the boy was lying across the wires, he managed somehow to remove the youth from the wires with a board or a large stick.

Then he picked his son up in his arms and held him, saying, "In the name of Jesus Christ and by the power and authority of the Holy Melchizedek Priesthood, I command you to live." The dead boy opened his eyes and talked with his father. He was taken to the University of Utah Medical Center. I believe it is these kinds of experiences that we have when we walk through this life with Him.

I believe also that it is the miracle of forgiveness. A couple drove all the way to Salt Lake City from their home in central California, came to my office, and said, "We need just half an hour with you. At conference you mentioned that every single major transgression must be confessed."

The man told me that on Monday after conference "my wife and I were sitting down for home evening, and not a word had been spoken. Then she said to me, 'Are you thinking what I'm

102

thinking?' And I said, 'Yes, I think I am.' She said, 'How soon should we leave?' And I said, 'Why not right now?'

And so they climbed into their car and drove sixteen hours to the Church Office Building. He said, "We have come to confess a major transgression. Forty-three years ago, before we were married, we committed fornication once. My father was the bishop of the ward, and he didn't ask us the questions when we applied for our temple recommends. We went to the stake president and he saw them signed by the bishop, so he didn't ask the questions. We went to the temple unworthily.

"While we were on our honeymoon we decided we would make it up to the Lord. We would give every particle of energy all of our lives to repent: there wasn't anything he could ask us to do that we wouldn't do. We would pay more than our share of tithing, more than our share of building fund. We would go forth and really serve. We wouldn't go to the temple during the next year because we weren't worthy." It was almost a self-imposed kind of repentance.

He said, "We've done everything we said we'd do. I've been a bishop and I've been on two high councils. My wife has been stake Relief Society president for six years. We know now—and I guess we've known all along, although we have repented—that we still had to confess."

Now, normally the General Authorities send people back to their bishops and stake presidents. They don't have to come to us. Every single member of the Church has a priesthood leader. But General Authorities are common judges, and so I called President Kimball on the phone and said, "President Kimball, I have a lovely couple in my office." I explained to him what the couple had just told me and added, "I feel that they've repented. Would you feel all right if I exercised my common judgeship and just simply closed this for these two wonderful people so they would not have to drive back to California and then go through this experience again?"

President Kimball said, "Are they still in your office?" "Yes." "Would you bring them right up."

Though that startled me, I said yes and then hung up the phone. I said to the couple, "President Kimball would like to see you in his office right now." The blood drained from their faces. I took them up to the twenty-fifth floor, where his office was at that time, and we walked back through the reception area to his secretary's office. There we were told, "The President is expecting you."

President Kimball got up from his desk and came to the door to meet us. I introduced him to the couple and said, "President, I need not stay. I'll run back downstairs. When you're finished call me, and I'll come right back up and get them." He said, "Bishop Featherstone, I want you to come in, too."

So we went into his office and sat down in front of his desk, while he went around behind the desk. For three or four minutes he visited with them tenderly and sweetly about some of the things he had in his office. Then he turned to the man and said, "Bishop Featherstone has told me about your problem. Have you suffered equal to the transgression?" In other words, It has been a major transgression; have you suffered?

The tears came to the man's eyes, and he said, "President, we think we have suffered many times more." President Kimball said, "Have you prayed for forgiveness?" And the man said, "I have prayed for forgiveness, and my wife has. We haven't offered a prayer in forty-three years in which we haven't asked for forgiveness."

Let me digress here just to say this: Do you know that the President of the Church is the only man on the face of the earth who can actually forgive on behalf of the Lord? President Kimball has said that he never uses this authority unless he really knows. The rest of us who are common judges forgive on behalf of the Church, as the Lord's agents.

After he talked to them and counseled with them, he said finally, "Would you feel all right if I'd come around and kneel down and have a prayer with you?" He came around from behind his desk, and we all knelt in prayer. Then President Kimball offered the prayer and said these words at the very beginning: "Heavenly Father, we love thee." As he said "We love thee," in a way I've never heard it said before, tears came to my eyes and streamed down my cheeks.

He went through the rest of the prayer, and I understood a little better then what an advocate is, because he pleaded for this couple. He felt that they had repented, but he needed to know.

Then finally, as he concluded his prayer and stood up, he came over, put his arm through mine, pulled me close to him, and asked me a question. You know, I don't know what the question was. I never answered it. All I know is that I turned to him with tears in my eyes and said, "President Kimball, I love you." And I did. Every particle of my heart and soul loved the man Spencer W. Kimball.

He then went over to the man and said to him as he shook his hand, "I want you to forgive yourself, and I want you to forgive your wife. I don't want you ever to think about it again. You are forgiven." The man put his head down on President Kimball's shoulder and sobbed. In a few moments President Kimball walked over to the woman, took both of her hands in his, and said, "I want you to forgive your husband, and I want you to forgive yourself. I want you to never think about it again. You are forgiven."

Now, I couldn't have had that experience had I not tried to walk in the Savior's footsteps. Every person who has had a similar experience has had it because he has tried to walk in His steps.

Who could forget the Canaanite woman who cried, as the Savior traveled between Sidon and Tyre with the disciples, "Have mercy on me, O Lord . . . my daughter is grievously vexed with a devil." The disciples said to the Master, "Send her away; for she crieth after us." The Savior, addressing not the woman but rather the disciples, replied, "I am not sent but unto the lost sheep of the house of Israel." And then the woman, knowing that they were talking about her, came to

105

him and worshipped him. She probably knelt down before him, maybe even taking his knees and laying her cheeks up against him, or looking up into his face, and said, "Lord, help me." And the Lord said something that at the time seemed so harsh: "It is not meet to take the children's bread, and to cast it to dogs."

Now, she could have stood up and said, "I'm not a dog, and I have some pride too, you know." And she could have worked her way away from the group. But she taught us one of the greatest lessons in humility. There is no question in my mind that the Savior knew exactly what her response would be. She said, "Truth, Lord: yet the dogs eat of the crumbs which fall from their masters' table." And he answered, "O woman, great is thy faith: be it unto thee even as thou wilt." The blessing was granted. (Matthew 15:22-28.)

We find also that when the Savior taught some extremely hard doctrine, the disciples two by two began to veer off, and they never walked again with him. Finally, all that were left were the Twelve Apostles, and he said to them, possibly with a heavy heart, "Will ye also go away?" And Peter said, "Lord, to whom shall we go? Thou hast the words of eternal life. And we believe and are sure that thou art that Christ, the Son of the living God." (John 6:66-69.)

Indeed, to whom shall we go if not to him? In whom could we put our trust? Where could we find that peace which surpasseth understanding? Where, when we've gone to the very limit, to the mountain too high and too wide and too deep in the earth to get across, where can we go when we need to be on the other side, except to him?

Now, I suppose we should think how this affects you and me. Well, we need to live a Christlike life. President Harold B. Lee said, "I came to a night, some years ago, when upon my bed I realized that before I could be worthy of the high place to which I had been called, I must love and forgive every soul that walked the earth. And in that time I came to know, and I received a peace, a direction, a comfort, and an inspiration that

106

told me things to come and gave me impressions that I knew were from a divine source." (*Stand Ye in Holy Places,* Deseret Book, 1975, p. 103.)

I wonder if in that hour President Lee didn't know that he would be the prophet, seer, and revelator of his church. I think, like him, that we must love and forgive every soul that walks the earth—a wayward son, a husband, a wife, maybe a divorced former companion, maybe someone who has offended us bitterly. If we would be Christlike, we must love and forgive every soul that walks the earth. Then are we entitled to that peace.

Elder James E. Talmage said that the cost is always the same for every single one of us as we accept Christ and him crucified. The cost of discipleship everlastingly and always will be the same. It is, simply, all that we have.

A modern prophet, President Kimball, has said, "We extend to every listener a cordial invitation to come to the watered garden, to the shade of trees, to unchangeable truth. Come with us to sureness, security, consistency. Hear the cooling waters flow. The spring does not dry. Come, listen to a prophet's voice and hear the words of God." (Long Beach, California, youth conference.)

I believe that we have in this generation those who are simply responding. The Lord has said, "My sheep hear my voice" (John 10:27), and they are coming to the shade, to the watered gardens, to the cool waters.

The great prophet Job wrote, "Oh that my words were now written! oh that they were printed in a book! That they were graven with an iron pen and lead in the rock for ever! For I know that my redeemer liveth, and that he shall stand at the latter day upon the earth: And though after my skin worms destroy this body, yet in my flesh shall I see God." (Job 19:23-26.)

And in this last day Joseph Smith and Sidney Rigdon, two great prophets, declared our gift to this generation: "And now, after the many testimonies which have been given of him, this is the testimony, last of all, which we give of him: That he lives!

107

For we saw him, even on the right hand of God; and we heard the voice bearing record that he is the Only Begotten of the Father—That by him, and through him, and of him, the worlds are and were created, and the inhabitants thereof are begotten sons and daughters unto God." (D&C 76:22-24.)

May our learning and education not only touch on the great truths of life, but more importantly, may they focus on the life of the Master, that we might hear his voice and follow in his sacred and holy footsteps.

Chapter Fifteen

Unconditional Love

Of all the examples of charity, the greatest is that of our Heavenly Father. He knows us, and he knows what we can do. And he loves us unconditionally, despite our weaknesses and shortcomings.

May I share with you a personal story. A bishop from a ward in a distant city came to see me one day and said, "We have a woman in our ward who would like to be excommunicated."

I said, "What's the problem? Have you talked to her?"

"Yes, we've tried to talk her out of it many times."

"Has the stake president talked to her?"

"Yes."

"What do you recommend?"

He said, "Well, we told her that we would like her to come to see you and talk to you, and if she still wanted to be excommunicated after she had the interview with you, we'd let her be excommunicated."

I answered, "Of course I'll see her." We made an appointment, and I want to tell you that I came to that interview with a great deal of prayer and a very humble heart. The woman came in, and I asked, "You are so-and-so?"

And she said, "Yes."

I said, "I have been expecting you."

She responded, "The only reason I am here is that my bishop said if I would come and talk to you I could be excommunicated after the interview. That's the only reason I'm here." Then she told me some of her experiences.

"When I was eighteen my mother died," she said, "and I had four younger brothers and sisters. I knew I couldn't start dating and getting serious about a fellow, so I didn't even look. Anything that started developing I just cut off. I took care of the family at home, and when the older of my young brothers was ready to go on a mission, I supported him. Then my second brother came along, and I supported him on his mission. They came back and eventually found companions and got married. My two sisters got married, and then all the family was raised. I was about thirty and I thought, 'Now I can get married.' A short time later I found the man, and we fell in love and got married.

"You know," she continued, "I believed that prayer is a one-way street. You just reported in, but you didn't dare ask for anything. All those years when I took care of and supported my brothers and sisters, I had a health problem. After I was married, my husband was called to be a seventy. We went to one of the seven presidents of the First Council of the Seventy, and he gave my husband a blessing as he ordained him. Then he said, 'I'd like to give you a blessing also.' I didn't ask for the blessing; he just volunteered it. He laid his hands on my head, and he told me something I didn't know until that day. He opened up a whole new dimension of life because he said, 'Do you know that when you pray you can ask God for things, and he will answer those prayers?' I hadn't known that before. That night, for the first time in my life I got down on my knees and started asking God for something.

"Then I decided that I had better make myself worthy. I was working then, and making more money than my husband. I started looking at myself and thinking my skirts were a little shorter than they ought to be, so I voluntarily lengthened them.

110

Then I thought that maybe I shouldn't be working. I didn't think the Lord would be pleased with my working, and we really didn't need both incomes, so I stopped working. We lived off my husband's income, and I managed his affairs for him at home. We paid our tithing all those years. At one time the bishop felt impressed to give me a blessing, and he promised me that I would have a man child, that our son would be a priesthood holder, and that he would do a great service for the Church. I didn't ask for the blessing; he volunteered it and gave it to me. So I expected that these promises would take place. We've been married five years now, but we have no children.

"Later on a member of the stake presidency gave me a blessing and promised me that my health would improve, but my health isn't any better. Do you know what it's like to have someone throw out a lifebuoy to you if you're drowning in the middle of the ocean? You swim and swim and finally get there, but when you reach out to take hold of the lifebuoy he pulls it away from you again. You swim farther, and you finally get there, but he always pulls it away. I don't believe in a God like that. I believe my bishop, and I believe in the stake presidency and in the president of the First Quorum of the Seventy, I know they are honest and upright men. But I don't believe in a God who would not keep his promises. I want to be excommunicated from the Church."

When I heard this sweet soul tell me her story, I sat and wept with her. I've never been through that. I've never had the Lord throw out a lifebuoy to me, let me swim toward it, and then, just as I got there, pull it away from me. I haven't been through that kind of test. As I heard this story, I thought in my heart, "Dear God, please, everything is riding on this interview. Help me to say the right thing today." After she had finished, I said, "You know, I really don't think you're really serious. You want to let him know that you just can't take any more, that you've had your limit of pressure."

She replied, "Yes, that's part of it."

Then I said, "But you know, you need to develop a Job-like

111

attitude. Job was a great soul, and he said, 'Though he [God] slay me, yet will I trust in him.' [Job 13:15.] If we have that kind of attitude, it doesn't matter what we go through, our reward is certain in the next life. You've put a time limit on the Lord. You've been married five years. What if in five years and six months you get pregnant, and then you have this child? What if a short time later your health comes? These things haven't happened, so you expect them now. What if it isn't for five years and nine months? It might be seven years, or fifteen years, or maybe not in this life. But I promise you, as surely as God is in heaven, that those promises made by righteous priesthood bearers will take place in your life. Now you don't want to be excommunicated, do you?"

She answered, "No, I really don't." The tears came a little faster then, and I wanted to say, "Would you like me to give you a blessing?" but I dared not do it.

She asked, "Bishop Featherstone, before I leave, would you please give me a blessing?" And so I gave her a blessing, and she left. I closed the door, went over and sat at the desk, and cried. Everything had hinged on that one interview, and God had been there. Why, at that very instant God had been answering her prayer, but she didn't even know it. He would continue to do so all through her life. You see, the God I worship has a thousand times more compassion than I have. If in my limited way I could see all that she had gone through and feel all that she had suffered, God would know much more than I ever could what suffering she should go through, the depth of it, and then at the right time he would not withhold those blessings from her. I hope you feel about that story the way I am trying to convey it. Sometimes we do feel as if God has thrown out the lifebuoy and then pulled it away from us. That isn't so. We must simply trust in him as Job did. "Though he slay me, yet will I trust in him."

Now I'd like to share some very personal experiences that, I hope, will help convey this message. When I was about seven or eight years old, a friend of mine, Spike Herzog, said to me as I was coming home from school one day, "Why don't you come to Primary with me?"

And I said, "Thanks, Spike, I'd like to." So I went to Primary with him, and after I had been there a short time, a year or so, I remember noticing a little box the Primary leaders checked off to show whether you were baptized or not. I hadn't been baptized, and I was nine years old by this time. I didn't know what baptism was, but I wanted that little box checked off. So I asked if I could be baptized. They said yes, and I was baptized.

During that time my dad was an alcoholic, and my mother wasn't a member of the Church. She has since joined and been through the temple, but then she wasn't even a member of the Church. I remember that on payday my mother would go over and stand against the mantel and look out the window up the street. She'd look and wait for the bus to come by that would drop Father off, I remember seeing her stand there from 4:30 to 6:30, 9:30, and even 10:30 at night. She never moved; she just stared out that window waiting for Dad to come. No food in the house, nothing. The family would gather together and say, "Let's go to bed. We can't add one featherweight of burden to our mother's heart." And so we'd go to bed hungry.

The next morning I would get up, and I couldn't tell but that she had been up all night. Mother would come to me, hand me a list, and say, "Vaughn, would you take this up to the store? Ask Mr. Parsons if we can charge these groceries, and tell him we don't have any food. Would you please do that?"

I would look up at her, and I'd want to say, "Mother, why do I always have to go? Can't you ask one of the other kids? Does it always have to be me?" But when I looked into her face and saw the heavy heart she had, I'd say, "I'll go." So I'd take the list, and I'd go out and get our old red wagon with the tires worn off and the rims worn flat. I would drag that wagon as slowly as a human being could possibly walk up the street. I'd get to the store and go in and walk around the aisles trying to avoid Mr. Parsons, who by the way (I didn't know at the time) was a high priest in our ward. Finally I'd walk up to him and hand him the

113

note, and he'd read it: "Dear Mr. Parsons, We don't have any food in the house. Would you mind charging fifty pounds of flour, a bucket of lard, some side pork, and a few other things? We promise to pay back every penny when we get some money. Thanks. [Signed] Mrs. Featherstone."

I'd see that great high priest and store owner look at the letter, then down at me, and tears would come to his eyes. He'd go get a big grocery cart, and then he would push it around the store and fill it up with all those things. He'd make out a charge slip and put it in the wagon, and I'd drag it home. I did that more times than I can tell you—embarrassed, bitterly embarrassed, every single time. I give the credit to my mother and older brothers in the family that we paid back every single penny that we ever borrowed from Mr. Parsons and from another grocer who gave us a charge account.

At about that same time we couldn't afford much clothing either. I had a pair of shoes that I'd wear to church. They weren't the best shoes. They had holes in the bottom sole, so I'd cut out pieces of cardboard and slide them in as an insole. When I went to church I would sit with both feet flat on the floor; I didn't want to raise one leg and have someone see "Quaker Oats" across the bottom of my shoe. I'd go off to church that way, and everything was fine until those shoes wore out. Then I didn't know what I would do. I remember it was Saturday, and I thought, "I've got to go to church. Over at church I am somebody. They really care about me." I remember thinking that through, and I went to a little box of shoes some neighbors had given us. I went through them, but I could find only one pair of shoes that would fit me. They were a pair of nurses' shoes. I thought, "How can I wear those? They'll laugh me to scorn over at church." And so I decided I wouldn't wear them, and I wouldn't go to church.

I went through that night, and the next morning I knew I had to go! I had to wear the nurses' shoes. There was a great attraction over at church. I had to go. I decided what to do. I would run over there very early and sit down close to the front

114

before anybody got there. I thought, "I'll put my feet back under the pew so no one can see them, and then I'll wait till everyone leaves. After they're gone I'll come running home half an hour later or something." That was my plan. I dashed over to church half an hour early, and it worked. Nobody was there. I put my feet back under the bench. Pretty soon everyone came in, and then all of a sudden someone announced: "We will now separate for classes." I had forgotten we had to go to class. I was terrified! The ushers came down the aisle, and as they got to our row, everybody got up and left. But I just sat there. I couldn't move. I knew I couldn't move for fear someone would see my shoes. The pressure was intense. That whole meeting seemed to stop and wait until I moved, so I had to move. I got up and followed the class downstairs.

I think I learned the greatest lesson I have ever learned in my life that day. I went downstairs to class, and the teacher had us sit in a big half-circle. Each of my shoes felt two feet in diameter. I can't tell you how embarrassed I was. I watched, but, do you know, not one of those eight- and nine-year-old children in that class laughed at me. Not one of them looked at me. No one pointed at my shoes. My teacher didn't look. I was watching everyone to see if anyone was looking at me, and I didn't hear a word of the lesson. When it was finally over I dashed home, went in the house, and thought to myself, "Thank goodness nobody saw them." How ridiculous! Of course they saw those nurses' shoes that I had to wear to church. But they had the fine instinct not to laugh. I guess the Lord knew that I had had all the pressure I could possibly take, that I couldn't take one particle more of pressure. I believe that all of us will find in our lives that some of our obstacles turn into advantages and great blessings.

My father was a great man when he was sober. Later on he and my mother were divorced. A short time after that I went one day to see my sweet mother. It was on the day Merlene and I were married. My older brother was the only one at the wedding from our side of the family. Afterwards, we went out to see my mother. I threw my arms around her and said, "I'd give anything in the world to have had you there with us this morning." She just couldn't make it. But bless that great champion's heart—she had stood by us as a family and had been our great defender in those bitter years. She never gave up on us; she always stuck with us. Can you begin to understand how I feel about her?

What I am saying is that if the Lord will take a scroungy little kid like that, who had to wear nurses' shoes to church and had to go and beg for groceries, and if he will make him a high councilor or a stake president or the second counselor in the Presiding Bishopric or a member of the First Quorum of the Seventy, can you believe what he would do for you?

We live in a wonderful dispensation, and some of the choicest spirits have been sent to earth in our time. Ours is a royal generation. Each one of us has problems to overcome, and each of us has much to offer. No matter how severe the handicaps, they can be overcome, if we each feel our real sense of worth and understand who we really are.

Index

Abram and Zimri, 14-15

Achievement, secrets of, 90

"Acres of Diamonds," 82-84

Adam, 96

Addiction of self-indulgence, 43-44

Administering to hospital patients, 29-30

Aged: problems of, 27; potential contributions of, 30, 32; caring for, 30-31

Alcoholic father, 113

Alder, Lorna Call, 36

Alma, 94-95

Aloi, Elder, 35-36

Antigonus, 18-19

Army, outnumbered, attacked and won, 18-19

Artist, satisfied, 91-92

Athletics, time limits in, 65

Author, knowing, makes book interesting, 93-94

Autograph book, 15

Baby, premature, blessing of, 101

Baptists, conversion of, 49

Baptist minister, daughter of, 49

Benson, Ezra Taft, 99

Bicycle, repairing, 53

Birds, classical music played to, 57

Birthday dollar, girl sent, to missionary brother, 12

Bombeck, Erma, 54-55

Book, dull, became interesting, 93-94

Branch president, concern of, for teenage boy, 9-10

Brande, Dorothea, 90

Brother and sister separated in orphan's home, 11

Brown, Hugh B., 77

Bus that tried to run taxi off road, 88-89

Canaanite woman begged Christ for blessing, 105-6

Cancer, man debilitated from, 101-2

Captain of soul, 51

Car, boy turned down, to serve mission, 37

Catholic, woman who had wanted to become, 48

Celestial room of Salt Lake Temple, 59

Charity: Mormon possessed, 203; Paul's discourse on, 304; Nephi possessed, 405; involves total commitment, 5; importance of developing, 6-7; is characteristic of true church, 7; involves doing what Christ would do, 14; acts of, may initially seem cruel, 17; exhibited by missionaries, 34, 41; involved in temple work, 58; greatest example of, is Heavenly Father, 109

Child abuse, 23-24

Children, offending, will bring judgment, 26

Church, man feared to join, because of poverty, 46

Clark, J. Reuben, 19-20

Clark, William Keith, 39

Classical music played to birds, 57

Clayton, Glen, 53

Climbing Mount Olympus, 69-70

Communication, charity enhances, 6

Compassion of Christ for afflicted, 26

Constitution of the United States, 20

Conwell, Russell, 82-84

Cooper, John, 15

Couple who confessed sin of fornication, 102-5

Crosses, carrying, with light hearts, 78-79

Curtis, Elder, 35-36

David, 66-67

Death of loved ones, 76-77

Delilah, 66

Dewey, John, 52

Diamonds, acres of, 82-84

Discipleship, cost of, 107

Discipline, men of, 18

Disneyland, war heroes brought to, 13-14

Doctors and nurses, salute to, 22-26

Dog, lesson in love taught by, 12

Eckstein, Dr. Gustav, 57

Edison, Thomas, 90

Electrocution, boy lived through, 102

Enduring to the end, 67

Enoch, 79, 96-97

Excommunication, woman asks for, 109-12

Failure: no reason for, 90; fear of, is worse than, 91

Family, responsibilities of, toward aged members, 30-31

Farmer's mother, praying with, 28-29

Father, letter from, about teenage son, 54

Ferrari, boy turned down, to serve mission, 37

Fiery furnace, youths cast into, 97-98

Forgiveness: charity involves, 6; President Kimball offered, to sinning couple, 102-5; of every soul on earth, 106-7

Fornication, couple confessed, to President Kimball, 102-5

General Authority, having an interview with, 70-71

Genius, 90

Gibran, Kahlil, 77

Gibson, Elder, 47-48

Gifford, Daniel, 37

God: love of, for man, 71, 79; has supreme interest in man, 81; sets greatest example of charity, 109; promises of, will be fulfilled, 112

Gospel of Jesus Christ, anchor provided by, 78

Grandparents, potential contributions of, 32
Granis, Elder, 37
Groceries, charging, 113-14
Guest, Edgar A., 32-33
Guttierrez, Brother, 45-46

Hamilton, Alexander, 90
Handicapped people, 22-23, 26
Henley, William Ernest, 50-51
Herzog, Spike, 112-13
Hilscher, Sister, 47-48
Holy Ghost, effect of, 5-6
Holy of Holies, 59
Home, poem about, 32-33
Hooks, tour guide offered to shake hands with, 13-14
Horn, Stephen, 33
Houses of the Lord, 58, 63
Humility, 71

Idleness, 19
Illness, lingering, 22-23
Impact teachers, 52-57
Importance, need for feeling of, 52
"Invictus," poem, 50-51

Jackson, Brother, 48
Jesus Christ: words of, 4-5; pure love of, 15-16; compassion of, for afflicted, 26; grandmother taught true love for, 32; sheep of, hear his voice, 41; offers rest to weary, 78; scriptures impart knowledge of, 94-95; woman touched clothes of, 100-101; Canaanite woman worshipped, 105-6; many disciples of, left him, 106
Job, 107, 112
Joens, Mr., 46-47

Kimball, Spencer W.: charity of, 7; sig-
nature of, in autograph book, 15; asked for bread and milk, 17-18; counsel from, to teachers, 55-56; service of, despite many illnesses, 99; couple confessed moral transgression to, 102-5; invites all to partake of truth, 107

Lazarus, 28
Lee, Harold B., 72, 76-77, 106-7
Lombardi, Vince, 38, 65, 69
Love: is essential to service, 8; involves stripping oneself of false pride, 10; absence of, 11; pure, of Christ, 15-16; absolute, of God, 71, 79
Lutheran church: young boy attended, 9-10; former minister of, 46-47

McKay, David O., 52
Memorization, value of, 1
Mercy, 22
Michelangelo, 90, 92
"Mike Will Come Back, Won't He?," 54-55
Military court, 64-65
Mission president: wife of, prayed for time to herself, 35; left prayer and blessing in home, 47
Missionaries: charity exhibited by, 34, 41; groceries left for, 35-36; letter from daughter of, 36; blessings promised to, 39
Missionary: sister of, sent birthday dollar to, 12; children of, supported her on mission, 37; was promised he would serve with General Authority, 37; who wanted to go home, 37-38; with dislocated shoulder, 38; with health problems, 42; who set record of proselyting hours, 43; preparing to become, 43; was promised ten baptisms, 44-45
Mitton, Claudia, 12-13

Monson, Thomas S., 62
Moral transgression, couple confesses, 102-5
Mormon, 2-3
Moroni, 2-3
Mortenson, Elder, 45
Moses, 97
Mother: poem about, 79-80; tribute to, 116
Mount Olympus, climbing, 69-70
Music, classical, played to birds, 57

Nebuchadnezzar, 97-98
Nephi, 4-5, 95-96
Nurses' shoes, 114-5
Nursing fathers and mothers, 22-23

Obstacles, 70, 91; praying for help in overcoming, 72; overcoming, by knowing who we are, 116
Old age, fears accompanying, 27
Orphan home, children separated in, 11

Paderewski, 90
Parents: accountability of, 24; responsibilities of, as teachers, 54
Parker, Joseph, 45
Patience, charity involves, 6
Paul, 1, 3-4
Perspective, 78
Petersen, Mark E., 77
Physical idiosyncracies, 89
Porter, Aldin, 53
Poverty: among elderly, 27; man put off baptism because of, 46; performing service in spite of, 100
Power in self-discipline, 18
Praying: with farmer's mother, 28-29; in former minister's home, 47; repetition in, 70; when faced with obstacles, 72
Premature baby, blessing of, 101
Pride, false, being stripped of, 6, 10

Priority, 78
Prisoner: who read Book of Mormon, 50; of war, military secrets revealed by, 64-65
Procrastination of repentance, 61, 67
Prophet, imagined prayer of, 59-60
Pure love of Christ, 15-16

Refiner's fire, 74
Relief Society president, 12-13
Repentance, 61-62
Repetition, sincere, vs. vain, 70
Respect for God's creations, 6
Richards, LeGrand, 34
Richards, Willard, 99
Rigdon, Sidney, 107-8
Rome, decline and fall of, 19
Romney, Marion G., 8, 19

Samson, 65-66
Schubert, 10
Schweitzer, Albert, 79
Scott, Sir Walter, 11-12
Scriptures: knowing Author of, 94; impart understanding of Christ, 94-95
Self-denial, 42-43
Self-indulgence, addictive nature of, 43-44
Self-pity, 78
Service; performing lesser, as well as greater, 2; charity involves, 6; men were born for, 8, 22
Shadrach, Meshach, and Abednego, 97-98
Sheaves, removing, to brothers' stacks, 14-15
Sheffield, Elder, 38-39
Shoes, nurses', 114-15
Simplicity, power of, 17-18
Smith, Joseph, 40, 99, 107
Snarr, Douglas, 84-89
Snow, Lorenzo, 74
Soul, captain of, 51

Spain, ambassadors from, 17

Speech impediment, young man with, 84-87

Spinola, 17

Success: poetic formula for, 90; recognizing potential for, 91

Suffering: purpose for, 74; need not be explained, 79; must eventually come, 80

Swimming pool, child drowned in, 25

Talmage, James E., 107

Tanner, Nathan Eldon, 19, 77, 80

Taxi driver, black, passenger sticks up for, 88-89

Teachers: potential power of, 52; failure of many, 53; President Kimball's admonitions to, 55-56

Temples: work in, is charitable, 58; description of, 58-59; preparing to enter, 62; are as perfect as possible, 62-63

Testimony: of Young Adult sister, 49; of Joseph Smith and Sidney Rigdon, 107-8

Testimony meeting, father joins family at, 50

Time: limits on, provide motivation, 65; for every purpose, 77

Tithing, 46, paid by widow, 100

Tranquilizers, 80

Trials: remaining faithful despite, 73-74, 78; every soul faces, 78-79

Truth shall penetrate whole earth, 40

Vance, Mike, 13

"Watcher, The," poem, 79-80

Weidel, Elder and Sister, 35

Widdemer, Margaret, 79-80

Widow, tithing of, 100

Widows, visiting, in affliction, 33, 99

Wife beating, 24-25

Women, virtuous, 25

Woodruff, Phoebe, 75-76

Woodruff, Wilford, 75-76

Words of Christ, 4-5

Young Adult sister, testimony borne by, 49

Youth: great generation of, 20-21; two great extremes facing, 44; are counseled to prepare to enter temple, 60-61

Zimri and Abram, 14-15

Though I speak with the tongues of men and of angels, and have not charity, I am become as sounding brass, or a tinkling cymbal.

2 And though I have the gift of prophecy, and understand all mysteries, and all knowledge; and though I have all faith, so that I could remove mountains, and have not charity, I am nothing.

3 And though I bestow all my goods to feed the poor, and though I give my body to be burned, and have not charity, it profiteth me nothing.

4 Charity suffereth long, and is kind; charity envieth not; charity vaunteth not itself, is not puffed up.

5 Doth not behave itself unseemly, seeketh not her own, is not easily provoked, thinketh no evil;

6 Rejoiceth not in iniquity, but rejoiceth in the truth;

7 Beareth all things, believeth all